Six Kings of
The American Pulpit

Six Kings of
The American Pulpit

BY

CLARENCE EDWARD MACARTNEY

D.D., LL.D., LITT.D.

PHILADELPHIA

THE WESTMINSTER PRESS

1942

COPYRIGHT, 1942, BY THE WESTMINSTER PRESS

PRINTED IN THE UNITED STATES OF AMERICA

FOREWORD

IN THE Stone Lectures for 1928 at Princeton Theological Seminary, Sons of Thunder, I spoke on the five great preachers of Great Britain and America. In book form these addresses were expanded into ten, and among the ten were six great American preachers: James Waddel, the blind preacher of Virginia; Peter Cartwright, the great circuit rider; Gilbert Tennent, Samuel Davies, Eliphalet Nott, and Lyman Beecher.

But the real kings of the American pulpit were not dealt with in the Stone Lectures. They were reserved for future treatment. That opportunity came in 1939, when I delivered the Smythe Lectures at the Columbia Theological Seminary of the Presbyterian Church in the United States. On that occasion I spoke on the six great figures of the American pulpit. One of them, William Jennings Bryan, was a layman; but all who heard him will agree that he takes his rank among the great preachers of America.

These addresses stirred the interest of the students and ministers who heard them, and they were also delivered to large congregations on Sunday *nights at my own church. The average person enjoys biography; and what biography is more stirring and fascinating than that of the mighty preachers of yesterday who proclaimed the glorious gospel of the blessed God and reasoned with men of righteousness and temperance and judgment to come?*

CLARENCE EDWARD MACARTNEY

CONTENTS

GEORGE WHITEFIELD

George Whitefield

ABOUT the year 1729, if you and I had entered the Bell Inn in Gloucester, England, where Robert Raikes, the printer, founded the first Sunday School, we should have seen a boy fifteen years of age, with a slight squint in one eye, clad in a blue apron, mopping the floor of the inn and drawing the ale and beer for his mother's customers. Within seven years this boy in the blue apron will be the most popular preacher in the world, and thousands will go to listen to him in town or in country whenever it is announced that he will preach.

George Whitefield was born December 16, 1714, at the Bell Inn, Gloucester. His father died when he was only two years old, leaving the faithful mother with the care of seven children, of whom George was the youngest. The ambitious mother sent him at the age of twelve years to the Gloucester Free Grammar School. There George soon distinguished himself by his memory and his elocution. Whenever the mayor came to visit the school, George was the boy chosen to make the speech. He would imitate the clergymen too, reading their prayers, and sometimes would gather the other boys about him and preach them a sermon. It was at Bristol, where he was visiting a brother, that he received his first serious religious impressions in a sermon at St. John's Church. His youth was full of spirit and play, but his later severe comments on his boyhood life are probably somewhat exaggerated. One offense seems to have been running into the meetinghouse of a learned and dissenting minister, Mr. Cole, and shouting out: "Old Cole! Old Cole!" He was one day asked by a member of Cole's congregation in what business he meant to be. His answer was: "A minister. But I would take good care never to tell stories in the pulpit like old Cole." But afterward, when he did his first preaching at Gloucester, Mr. Cole went to hear him and noted with pleasure his use of stories and anecdotes.

Whitefield's inability to get along with the wife of a married brother who had taken the Bell Inn resulted in his visit to Bristol, and after that in his going back to his old schoolmaster at St. Mary De Crypt, where he fitted himself for Oxford, having secured through his mother's enterprise a position as servitor at Pembroke College. The difference he had with his brother's wife Whitefield afterward recorded as God's way of "forcing me out of the public business and calling me from drawing wine for drunkards to draw water out of the wells of salvation for the refreshment of his spiritual Israel."

Whitefield entered Oxford when he was eighteen, in the year 1733. One of the books which influenced his life was Law's *Serious Call to the Unconverted*. Another was a book given him by his new-found friend Charles Wesley, *The Life of God in the Soul of Man*. Whitefield writes of this experience: "I never knew what true religion was till God sent me that excellent treatise. Not till then did I know that I must be a new creature. Like the woman of Samaria, I wrote letters to my relations telling them that there was such a thing as a New Birth. They thought I was going beside myself." It was this doctrine of the new birth, the necessity and the possibility of it, that erelong was to be the burden of Whitefield's apostolic preaching.

It is a Sunday evening at Oxford. Through the streets of the hoary town wander groups of students, and rollicking songs are rolling out on the night air. In Lincoln College the apartments are filled with other students, some studying, others drinking, singing, gambling. But in one room we come upon a group which contrasts strangely with all the others. Near a table where a lighted candle sheds its glow on the page sits a young Fellow of Lincoln, about twenty-six years of age, slight, fair, blue-eyed, with a certain winsome beauty in his face. He is reading from the New Testament to the group of students around him. After the reading they speak of their life during the past week and then kneel together in prayer. Other students returning from the gin houses come noisily up the hallway and, hearing the sound of the earnest voices in prayer, pound on the door with their fists and shout as they pass: "The Bible bigots!" "The Holy Club!" "The Bible Moths, the Methodists, are at it again!" But the men on their knees continue in prayer. Neither those who are praying nor those who are scoffing can have any conception of the energies which are being created that night in that room. The songs of one of those kneeling men, Charles Wesley, are to sing themselves around the world and become the battle music of the greatest religious reformation since the sixteenth century. The spiritual experience of his brother John will open a new highway over which the weary feet of men may pass to the light and peace of heaven; and the voice of another, the young man with the large head and heavy neck, on whose face the play of the candlelight betrays recurrent waves of strong emotion, is to sound like a silver trumpet through the busy streets of London, over the moors of Scotland, and in the pits and quarries of Cornwall, in the savannas of Georgia, in the towns of Pennsylvania and New Jersey, on the banks of the Delaware, and in the forests of New England.

It was a great day for George Whitefield when he first made the acquaintance of Charles Wesley, and through him of the other members of that group who were known as "Methodists." Charles Wesley, forty years afterward, thus wrote of the meeting:

"Can I the memorable day forget,
When first we by Divine appointment met?
Where undisturbed the thoughtful student roves,
In search of truth, through academic groves;
A modest, pensive youth, who mused alone,

Industrious the frequented path to shun,
An Israelite without disguise or art,
I saw, I loved, and clasped him to my heart,
A stranger as my bosom-friend caressed,
And unawares received an angel-guest."

Whitefield adopted the life of the Methodists, meeting with them for prayer and study, taking the sacrament every Sunday, and visiting the sick and the prisoners. At first he says he was sort of ashamed of his association with them, and was glad to go among them, like Nicodemus, "only by night." After trying spiritual experiences, and many temptations of Satan, Whitefield came to a joyous experience as a follower of Christ and was filled with a desire to preach the everlasting gospel. On a visit to Gloucester in 1735, the bishop of Gloucester, Bishop Benson, sent for Whitefield and told him that he had good reports of him and his character, and although Whitefield was only twenty-one years of age, would ordain him whenever he was ready.

The Sunday following his ordination he preached his first sermon in the Church of St. Mary De Crypt. His theme was, "The Necessity and Benefit of Religious Society." Before preaching the sermon he had sent it to a minister not far away, to prove to him, he

says, "how unfit he was for the office of a preacher."
After a week the minister returned it to him with a
guinea, saying that he had divided the sermon into
two parts and preached it morning and evening to
his own congregation. A great throng filled the
church on that June Sunday in 1736 when Whitefield preached his first sermon. He says he was over-
awed at first, but was comforted by a sense of the
divine Presence, and had the great advantage of having done public speaking when he was a boy at
school and at the university. "As I proceeded," he
wrote, "I perceived the fire kindled, till at last
though so young, and amidst a crowd of those who
knew me in my infant, childish days, I trust I was
enabled to speak with some degree of gospel authority. Some few mocked; but most of those present
seemed struck."

A complaint was made to the bishop of Gloucester
that Whitefield's sermon had driven fifteen people
mad. The bishop sagely remarked that he hoped the
madness would last until the next Sunday.

After this first sermon, Whitefield returned to
Oxford for a season, and then engaged in occasional
preaching at Bristol and the Tower of London. He
seems to have had immediate and extraordinary suc-

cess, and wherever it was announced that he was to preach vast throngs resorted to hear him. In London he preached as many as nine times in the week, and long before daybreak the streets were crowded with people with lanterns in their hands going to hear him reason with them of righteousness and temperance and judgment to come. Very early, Whitefield set for himself a standard of unremitting labor. "I had rather wear out than rust out. No nesting on this side of eternity," was his reply to those who implored him to spare his strength. The sermon which was used of God to begin an awakening in many of the places where he preached was the sermon on "The Nature and Necessity of Our Regeneration," or, "New Birth in Jesus Christ."

In 1737, Whitefield went out to the newly established colony of Georgia to take the place of Wesley as preacher and chaplain at Savannah. It was Wesley's call that made Whitefield feel sure that God wanted him to go to Georgia: "What if thou art the man, Mr. Whitefield? Do you ask me what you shall have? Food to eat and raiment to put on, a house to lay your head in such as your Lord had not, and a crown of glory that fadeth not away." "Upon reading this," says Whitefield, "my heart leaped within me." It was a turning point in his history.

After a few months in Georgia, Whitefield returned to England to receive full ordination as a priest and to gather funds for the orphanage which he planned to establish in Georgia, the maintenance of which was henceforth a cause dear to his heart, and for which his golden eloquence gathered in America and Britain large sums of money.

When he returned to England he found that a prejudice against the Wesleyan movement had closed practically all the churches to him. It was this fact that made Wesley and Whitefield the great field preachers. Because all doors were closed to him in Bristol, except the doors of the prison, Whitefield went out into the open and preached to the colliers of Kingwood. About two hundred were present the first day. Whitefield said: "I thought it might be doing the service of my Creator, who had a mountain for his pulpit and the heavens for his sounding board, and who when the gospel was refused by the Jews, sent his servants into the highways and hedges."

The news of Whitefield's extraordinary eloquence, and his unheard-of procedure, preaching outside a church, soon spread, and the next time he spoke at Kingwood a congregation of upward of ten thousand had assembled. Whitefield recorded that the first discovery of how he affected them was when he saw the "white gutters made by the tears which plentifully fell down their black cheeks as they came out of the coalpits." Invited by Whitefield to come down to help him in his work at Bristol, John Wesley was shocked at his first experience in an open air meeting. He says, "I could scarce reconcile myself at first to his strange way of preaching in the fields, of which he set me the example on Sunday, having been all my life till very lately so tenacious of every point relating to decency and order that I should have thought the saving of souls almost a sin if it had not been in a church." His brother Charles was even more opposed to such a procedure, and it was only after they had cast the lot that it was determined that John should go down to help Whitefield. The Sunday after he heard Whitefield preach, Wesley climbed to the top of a grassy mound outside Bristol, and looking down into a sea of grimy, upturned faces, took for his text the prophetic words of Christ: "The Spirit of the Lord is upon me, because he hath anointed me to preach the gospel to the poor; he hath sent me to heal the brokenhearted, to preach deliverance to the captives, and recovering of sight to the blind, to set at liberty them that are bruised, to preach the acceptable year of the Lord."

In 1739, Whitefield returned again to America, with the purpose of establishing his orphanage at Bethesda in Georgia, although he had given up the idea of being a settled preacher in the church at Savannah. "The whole world," he wrote to a friend, "is now my parish. Wherever my Master calls me I am ready to go and preach his everlasting gospel."

It was on this visit to America that Whitefield made the acquaintance of Benjamin Franklin. The freethinking Franklin printed Whitefield's sermons, of which great numbers were sold. Franklin thought that their publication did injury to Whitefield's reputation, which, he said, depended principally upon his wonderful voice and delivery. Whitefield was a guest at Franklin's house. In replying to an invitation Franklin had sent him at Boston, Whitefield said, "If you make that offer for Christ's sake, you will not miss the reward." To which the philosopher answered: "Don't let me be mistaken. It was not for Christ's sake, but for your sake." Whitefield often prayed for his host's conversion, "but," says Franklin, "never had the satisfaction of believing that his prayers had been answered."

Franklin used to stand on the outskirts of the throngs listening to Whitefield on Market Street, Philadelphia, and estimate the size of the crowd. He said that he used to doubt what he had read about generals haranguing whole armies, but when he found that Whitefield could preach to thirty thousand people and be heard by them all, he was less inclined to be skeptical.

Franklin was interested in Whitefield's projects for the establishment of an orphanage, but thought, perhaps correctly, that the orphanage should be built in Philadelphia, and not in the new and thinly populated colony of Georgia. For this reason Franklin determined not to contribute to the orphanage. Soon after his decision he was listening to Whitefield preach, and knowing that he would take a collection for the orphanage at the end of the sermon, resolved that he should have nothing from him. "I had in my pocket a handful of copper money, three or four silver dollars, and five pistoles in gold. As he proceeded I began to soften, and concluded to give the copper. Another stroke of his oratory made me ashamed of that and determined me to give the silver, and he finished so admirably that I emptied my pockets into the collection dish, gold and all." Franklin goes on to tell that on the same occasion there was a man, Hopkinson, who had taken the precaution to empty his pockets before he came to the church, but as the great preacher struck fire he felt so strong an inclination to give that he asked a neighbor who stood near him to lend him some money. The neighbor was one of the few not affected by the preacher's plea, for he answered, "Any other time, friend Hopkinson, I would lend thee freely, but not now, for thee seems to be out of thy right senses."

Although Franklin did not approve of the establishment of the orphanage in Georgia, he nevertheless accepted an appointment as a member of the board of trustees. In his newspaper for November, 1739, Franklin tells of the extraordinary crowds to which Whitefield preached: seven thousand at Chester, five thousand at Wilmington, two thousand at New Castle, eight thousand at White Plague Creek, where half the congregation had come on horseback and stood listening in the pouring rain. When we read of these vast assemblies, we must remember the thinly populated country and the great distances that Whitefield's hearers had to traverse. Franklin was amazed at the way in which people thronged to hear Whitefield preach, and speculated on his influence on the hearers and their admiration and respect for the preacher, notwithstanding that he told them that they were half beasts and half devils. He noted too the change in the life of the people, and how it seemed to him as if the whole world were growing religious, so that one could not walk through the town of an evening without hearing everywhere the singing of psalms and hymns.

Whitefield and the Wesleys had a serious dispute over Calvinism, a dispute which at one time threatened to disrupt their memorable friendship. Perhaps the Wesleys were the aggressors, rather than Whitefield. Fortunately, a break was averted, and their dispute as to Calvinism and Arminianism was an illustration of how the lines which separate need not alienate. An amusing anecdote is related of John Wesley and Whitefield in connection with this theological difference. On one occasion, after a hard day's labor for the Lord, the two men slept together in the same bed. Whitefield, well spent, threw himself down on the bed at once without a prayer. "George," said Wesley in a reproachful tone, "is that your Calvinism?" and then knelt down by the side of the bed to pray. In the middle of the night Whitefield awoke and found Wesley fast asleep on his knees by the bedside. Awakening him, he said, "John, is that your Arminianism?"

On one of those visits to America, Whitefield formed the acquaintance of the Tennents, William Tennent, the founder of the Log College on the Neshaminy Creek, and Gilbert Tennent, the fiery preacher of New Brunswick and the chief leader in the movement which in 1741 led to the schism in the Presbyterian Church of the Old Side and the New Side. The college established on the Neshaminy ultimately became Nassau College at Princeton, New Jersey. Whitefield helped to raise funds in Great Britain for Princeton, and also for Dartmouth College. Of Princeton he wrote that "it was a blessed nursery, one of the purest, perhaps, in the universe, where the worthy president and three tutors are all bent upon making the students both saints and scholars." Together with Jonathan Edwards and the Tennents, Whitefield was one of the chief voices of the Great Awakening, the remarkable revival of the fourth decade of the eighteenth century. When we estimate his contribution to American religious life, we must remember that Great Awakening. To a certain degree, also, Whitefield's preaching exerted a political influence. "Impetus was given to education, schools and colleges were established; a social consciousness emerged, and philanthropic and missionary work was initiated." The preaching of Whitefield, with the throngs which waited upon it, gave a common religious emotion to the American people and broke down denominational and colonial barriers. Thus the great religious movement and awakening in which Whitefield played so important a part prepared the way for the American Revolution.

In November, 1769, Whitefield came to America for the last time, his thirteenth crossing of the Atlantic Ocean. He landed at Charleston and proceeded northward to Philadelphia, New York, and New England. It was on this last tour that he preached to a man about to be hanged. After the sermon he walked with him half a mile to the gallows and went up into the hangman's cart with him. Before the trap was sprung the murderer made a testimony for Christ.

In September Whitefield was in Boston. He had been ill, but after riding sixty miles felt much better. His prayer was not for health, but, "O for a warm heart!" After preaching at Portsmouth he set out for Boston, stopping at Exeter, where he preached to a great multitude his last sermon. The text was II Cor. 13:5: "Examine yourselves, whether ye be

26

in the faith." The mark of death was already upon him, and not for several minutes after he stood on the pulpit platform was he able to find utterance. One of the ministers there said to him, "Sir, you are more fit to go to bed than to preach." "True, sir," answered Whitefield, and then, looking up to heaven, he gave utterance to that beautiful and familiar saying: "Lord Jesus, I am weary in thy work, but not of thy work."

At the home of Mr. Parsons, the minister at Newburyport, he went to his room after evening prayers, and at 2:00 A.M. awoke gasping for breath. To his companion and attendant he said that he hoped two or three days' ride and a pulpit sweat would set him up again. But the great rider for Christ had taken his last ride. He expired at 6:00 A.M., September 30, 1770, and was buried before the pulpit in the Presbyterian Church. An elaborate epitaph was inscribed on a memorial in Tottingham Court Chapel. But when we think of his epitaph it is the one that he himself had prepared which comes to our mind:

"Here lies George Whitefield. What sort of a man he was, the Great Day will discover."

27

A century and threescore and twelve years have passed since Whitefield died at Newburyport. But in these years no preacher has arisen like him, as no preacher like him had arisen before him. Before he made his last trip to America, a friend had asked him whom he would like to have preach his memorial sermon in case of his death in America. His answer was: "John Wesley. He is the man." When the news of Whitefield's death in America came to London, a woman follower of Whitefield went up to John Wesley after a service in the Foundry and, referring to the controversy between the Wesleys and Whitefield over the subject of Calvinism, said, "Mr. Wesley, do you expect to see George Whitefield in heaven?" Wesley answered, "No." "Ah, I was afraid you would say that," responded the woman. Then Wesley, lifting his head, said, "Wait, madam; when I get to heaven, George Whitefield will be so near to the throne that a poor sinner like me will never get a sight of him!"

No Christian minister ever preached continually to such multitudes and for so many years as George Whitefield did, and probably no preacher turned so many sinners to repentance. As John Wesley said in his memorial sermon: "What an honor

28

hath God put upon his servant! Have we read or heard of any person since the apostles who testified the gospel of the grace of God through so widely extended a place, through so large a place of the habited world? Have we read or heard of any person who called so many thousands, so many myriads of sinners to repentance? Above all, have we read or heard of any who has been a blessed instrument in His hands of bringing so many sinners from darkness to light and from the power of Satan unto God?"

This remarkable herald of the everlasting gospel was a man of about average height, and, up to the age of forty, spare and thin. After that, in spite of his endless journeys on horseback, he became somewhat portly. In person he was always scrupulously neat and cleanly. One of his best portraits shows him in pulpit gown and band, his face round and mobile, the left eye with a slight squint. Those who mocked him spoke of him as "Dr. Squintum."

Had we heard him, the thing that would have struck us most at first was his extraordinary voice. David Garrick, the famous actor, said he would give a hundred guineas if only he could say, "Oh," as

Mr. Whitefield did. Garrick also said that had Whitefield been disguised, he might have made men weep or tremble by the varied utterance of the word "Mesopotamia."

We should have been struck too with the deep earnestness and emotion of the preacher. It has been asked whether if Whitefield came back to earth he would get a hearing now. Would he be popular today as he was a century and three quarters ago? No doubt the throngs would not be so numerous, not because of the difference in the preacher or the people, but because of a difference in the times. There were no moving pictures, no great football games, to attract the multitudes then as there are today. But holy energy will always be popular, and always impressive, too, will be the deep earnestness of a man like Whitefield. A bishop once asked the actor Betterton why the preachers produced so little effect. "My lord," answered Betterton, "I can assign but one reason. We players speak of things imaginary as though they were real, and too many clergymen speak of things real as though they were imaginary." Richard Baxter's couplet could well be put into the mouth of George Whitefield, for that was the way he always preached:

"I preached as never sure to preach again,
And as a dying man to dying men."

Whitefield was an emotional preacher in the highest sense of the word. Those who heard him frequently said that he rarely preached a sermon without weeping. Winter said of him that he wept, stamped, shouted loudly and passionately, and was frequently so overcome that some seconds would elapse before he could recover himself. In one of his own sermons Whitefield said, "You blame me for weeping; but how can I help it when you will not weep for yourselves though your immortal souls are on the verge of destruction?"

When Whitefield preached at Northampton for Jonathan Edwards, who had cautioned him about his extreme utterances and his severe judgments on other ministers, the great thinker was seen weeping silently while the great preacher reasoned of righteousness and temperance and judgment to come.

Whitefield's printed sermons give not the slightest intimation of the marvelous effect of his preaching. The published sermons, however, had a remarkable popularity, and were frequently read at church gatherings and greatly used by the Holy Spirit.

Franklin, who published them, gave it as his opinion that the published sermons did Whitefield more harm than good because there was nothing in them to remind the people of the preacher's power. Probably Whitefield or some editor had gone through them and deleted the anecdotal or dramatic passages. I have searched in vain through several volumes of the printed sermons for a single anecdote, and yet it is well known that his use of anecdotes was one of the characteristics of his preaching.

Whitefield was often dramatic. His preaching was acting in the noblest sense. Here was one preacher who could never be charged with preaching great realities as if they were fiction. Sometimes when preaching in a section where the courts were in session Whitefield would liken himself to a judge about to sentence a prisoner. On one occasion he even put a black cap on his head. "Sinner, I must do it! I must pronounce sentence! Depart from me! I never knew you!" And the dread sentence would be pronounced with stifled sobs. When he preached on Peter going out into the night, weeping bitterly, after his denial of Jesus, he always had a fold of his gown ready in which to hide his face.

Whitefield was a master at description, as indeed

most popular preachers have been. He could describe the sufferings of Christ in a way that answered the end of real scenery; and, as though Gethsemane were within sight, he would say, stretching out his hand: "Look yonder! What is it I see? It is my agonizing Lord!" Some of the Scotch Presbyterians objected to this, and Ralph Erskine wrote of his preaching: "They see a beautiful and glorious person presented to their imagination, or to their bodily eye. What a devil instead of a Christ is this!"

Whitefield made full use of the apostrophe, so little used in any form of speech and writing today. His most moving passages, Southey wrote of him in his life of Wesley, "were bursts of passion, like jets of a geyser when the spring is in full play." David Hume, who said it was worth going twenty miles to hear Whitefield, saw one of these geyserlike jets of spontaneous passion and emotion. He says: "Once after a solemn pause he thus addressed his audience. 'The attendant angel is just about to leave the threshold of the sanctuary and to ascend to heaven. And shall he ascend and not bear with him the news of one sinner among all this multitude reclaimed from the error of his ways? Stop, Gabriel! Stop! ere you enter the sacred portals, and yet carry with you the news of one sinner converted to God!' "

He was always quick and ready to make use of any passing incident. On one occasion a young man had mounted a tree near his field pulpit to mock at the preacher. But Whitefield addressed himself to him, and, likening him to Zacchaeus, invited him like Zacchaeus to come down out of the tree and receive Christ into his soul. Sometimes he made personal appeals. Once he saw in his congregation the actor Shutter, who played the part of the Rambler. Fixing his eyes on him, Whitefield cried out, "And thou poor Rambler, who hast long rambled from Him, come you also. Oh, end your rambling by coming to Jesus!" It had a deep effect upon Shutter, who said to Whitefield afterward: "I thought I should have fainted. How could you serve me so?"

In a day when nearly every preacher read hour-and-a-half-long discourses, Whitefield preached without notes. This was something new, and a mighty asset to him. When he was attacked by the professors at Harvard on this ground, that he preached without notes and that no strong argument could be managed in that way, Whitefield answered: "Indeed, gentlemen, I love to study and delight to meditate.

34

Preaching without notes costs as much if not more close and solitary thought, as well as confidence in God, than with notes." He repeated his sermons over and over again, taking from them the weak and ineffective passages and retaining only those parts which by trial had been found effective. Foote and Garrick, the actors, who frequently went to hear him, thought that he was not at his best until he had preached a sermon forty or fifty times. Franklin too said that the sermons improved greatly by repetition.

The printed sermons, although they give no slightest hint of the secret of Whitefield's power as a preacher, show an orderly method and lucid thinking. There is always a clear exposition of the passage from which the text is taken; then a statement of his proposition, and the several points to be brought out; and always at the end a moving appeal. Indeed, the preaching is personal from beginning to end. In the introduction to the sermon on "Justification," I Cor. 6:11, Whitefield says, "It has been objected by some who dissent from—nay, I may add by others also, who actually are friends to— the present ecclesiastical establishment, that the ministers of the Church of England preach themselves and not Christ Jesus, the Lord; that they entertain their people with mere lectures of mere morality, without declaring to them the glad tidings of salvation by Jesus Christ." There is no doubt that that was true of a large part of the preaching of Whitefield's day. His preaching had, therefore, the great advantage of novelty when he presented the great doctrines of redemption, and not only described them and declared them, but presented them to the conscience and to the heart of his hearer. An example of his homiletic style is his sermon on an "almost Christian," Acts 26:28. The following is the outline:

First, What is meant by an "almost Christian." He defines an "almost Christian" as one who halts between two opinions, and wavers between Christ and the world.

Second, The reasons why so many are no more than "almost Christians." These are, that so many set out with false notions of religion, a servile fear of man, a reigning love of money, and the love of pleasure and instability of temper.

Third, The folly of being no more than an "almost Christian." It is folly because it is ineffectual to salvation, and also prejudicial to the salvation of others. It is ingratitude to Christ who shed his precious blood. Then comes the appeal, and "word or two of exhortation."

Except in the early days of his career, Whitefield seems to have made little or no preparation for the pulpit. His friends and companions said he had no set time and no systematic study, except in the early period of his ministry. The parts of the sermons that he wrote were the least effective, and his fame rested on spontaneous outbursts, which to a large degree are precluded by the written or memorized sermon. Sometimes before preaching, he would seclude himself for an hour or two with Clark's Bible, Henry's *Commentary*, and Cruden's *Concordance*, those three old and tried friends of the preacher. Whitefield used to say that the best preparation for preaching was preaching every day. For great periods of his life he preached several times a day, and lamented when conditions of health put him on what he called "short allowance"—once every day and three times on Sunday.

Whitefield frequently addressed great multitudes with no preparation at all except the best preparation about which he used to speak, constant preaching. "Sometimes," he says, "when twenty thousand people were before me I had not in my apprehension a word to say, either to God or to them. But I was never totally deserted, and was frequently, for to deny it would be lying against God, so assisted that I knew by happy experience what our Lord meant by saying, 'Out of his belly shall flow rivers of living water.' "

There were favorite sayings which he repeated over and over again in the pulpit. One of them was the noble apostrophe of Jeremiah, which Whitefield used with great power: "O earth, earth, earth, hear the word of the Lord"!

There are many recorded instances of the extraordinary effect of his preaching upon his hearers. One is the already related incident of the reluctant Franklin, who had gone to the service determined to give nothing but emptied all the money in his pockets into the collection dish. Another is that of his preaching one time in New York, when he described a ship dismasted and thrown on her beam-ends by the storm. He cried out, "What next?" Several sailors were in the gallery, and, rising to their feet, they exclaimed with one voice in their excitement: "The long boat! Take to the long boat!" Another is that of the fastidious Chesterfield, who instructed his own son in the art of seduction. Sitting in Lady Huntingdon's pew one Sunday at White-field's Tabernacle, Chesterfield heard him liken the sinner to a blind beggar passing along a dangerous road near a cliff. The beggar's little dog gets away from him near the edge of the cliff, and he is left to explore the dangerous path with his iron-shod staff. Once he comes to the very edge of the preci-pice, where he drops his staff into the abyss. All unconscious of his danger, the blind man stoops down to reach for his staff and plunges forward over the edge of the precipice. Leaping to his feet, to avert if possible the catastrophe, Chesterfield cried out: "Great God, he's gone!"

We have spoken thus far of the man and his method, his manner and personality. Now we come to something more important, the spirit that was in him and the message which he proclaimed. In a single sentence you can say that the message of Whitefield was regeneration, the new birth. When Whitefield was a student at Oxford, Charles Wesley put into his hands a book by Henry Scougal, *The Life of God in the Soul of Man*. This gave him his first idea of the religious life as a real union with God, and for that great power and blessing he strove until he had it. The life of God in his soul, the new birth, a consciousness of regeneration, was undoubtedly the power back of Whitefield's apostolic preaching. He proclaimed the majesty of the soul.

Whitefield's sermon on "Regeneration," II Cor. 5:17—"If any man be in Christ, he is a new creature"—presents his view on this great theme. He commences by saying, what is almost equally true again today, that multitudes of those who accept the great articles of the Christian creed know nothing of the doctrine of regeneration. He has interesting illustrations of what it means to be a new creature. As a piece of gold that was once in the ore, after it has been purified and polished, is a new piece; and as a bright glass that has been covered with filth, and then wiped so that it becomes transparent and clear, is a new glass; or as Naaman when he was recovered of his leprosy, so that "his flesh came again like unto the flesh of a little child," could be spoken of as a new man; so our souls, although still the same as to essence, when they are purged, purified, and cleansed from their natural dross, filth, and leprosy by the blessed influence of the Holy Spirit, can be truly said to be made anew. As for the difficulties in the way of the doctrine of regeneration, Whitefield uses the statement of our Lord about the wind, how we hear the sound thereof but cannot know "whence it cometh, and whither it goeth." Thus, if we cannot understand natural things like the wind, how much less can we understand the invisible workings of the Holy Spirit.

A strong argument for the necessity of the new birth Whitefield draws from the fact that man as a sinner, unless completely remade, can never dwell in the presence of God. He makes a strong point, too, of how man, unless born again, is unfit for the Kingdom of heaven. He asks what delight the deaf can have in the most harmonious music, or the blind in the most beautiful picture, or the tasteless palate in the richest dainties, or the filthy swine with the finest garden of flowers. In urging upon his hearers that the outward forms of religion, and even taking delight in sermons, are not sufficient, he makes an interesting comment on Herod, who heard good sermons gladly, referring, of course, to how Herod delighted to hear John the Baptist preach, but did not repent.

One difficulty about the doctrine of the new birth has perhaps presented itself to many preachers. They sometimes hesitate to emphasize it lest it dis-

courage men from hoping to be Christians, or dis-
count the sincere efforts they have already made in
the Christian life. Whitefield did not feel that difficulty, and in the conclusion of his sermon stressed
the fact that although regeneration is a great and
difficult work, it is not impossible. It can be done
with the help of God, and is gloriously worth every
sacrifice which it involves. Even here, a new creature as a child of God will be the inheritor, and ere
long, the actual possessor, of the Kingdom of God.

One of Whitefield's most graphic and dramatic
sermons is that on "Peter's Denial," Matt. 26:75.
Here we have Whitefield not so much the proclaimer
and expounder of the great doctrines as the describer
of sin and temptation, the emotions of the human
heart, and the appealer to man's love for Christ
and Christ's love for man. He divides the sermon
into three parts: the steps that led to Peter's fall,
the fall itself, and Peter's recovery.

After a dramatic description of the scene in Gethsemane, there follows the account of Peter's sleep.
That is the first step in his fall. The second step
is when he follows Jesus afar off. He sulks behind
and keeps on purpose at a distance lest he should be

accounted one of his followers: "Peter! Peter! Did I not know how prone my own deceitful heart is to go astray from the great Shepherd and Bishop of our souls, I should now begin to say: 'Fie upon thee! Fie upon thee!' Hadst thou kept close to thy Lord, thou mightest have been sheltered safely under his almighty wings. But how canst thou avoid falling, and that foully too, when thou beginnest thus to be ashamed of thy glorious Master?"

Then comes the third step in Peter's fall. He goes into the high priest's palace and sits with the servants: "O Peter! my blood begins now to run almost cold within me. I tremble for thee more than ever. What canst thou propose for thyself, or what bad thing may we not expect to hear of thee when sitting in such sorry company?"

The next step in Peter's fall is when he first denies Christ by a kind of equivocation: "Surely the way of sin is downhill. One step leads to another. At first he only denied what was said to him by a kind of equivocation: 'I know not what thou sayest.' Now he grows bolder and denies with an oath: 'I know not the man.' Surely it is high time for the cock to crow. Hark! The cock does crow, not only

once but twice; but all in vain. Fallen as this great
man is, he must still fall lower. Satan is now about
to give him the last and most fatal thrust." Then
comes the account of the third denial, and Peter's
cursing and swearing: "And now, Satan, thou hast
gained thy point. A great man, through too much
self-confidence, spiritual pride, spiritual sloth, and
too great intimacy with some of thy children, is
fallen indeed."

After a moving description of what was in that
look with which Jesus "looked upon Peter," the
great preacher described Peter's remorse and agony:
"Alas! it is too big to speak. But his tears, his briny,
bitter, penitent tears, plainly bespeak this to the language of his awakened soul. 'Alas! where have I
been? On the Devil's ground? With whom have I
been conversing? The Devil's children. What is this
that I have done? Denied the Lord of Glory with
oaths and curses, denied that ever I knew him. And
now whither shall I go, or where shall I hide my
guilty head? I have sinned against light, I have
sinned against repeated tokens of his dear distinguishing and heavenly love. I have sinned against
repeated warnings, resolutions, promises, and vows.

I have sinned openly in the face of the sun, in the presence of my Master's enemy, and thereby have caused His name to be blasphemed. How can I think of being suffered to behold the face or, much less to be employed by, the ever blessed Jesus any more. O Peter! thou hast undone thyself! Justly mayest thou be thrown aside like a broken vessel. God, be merciful to me a sinner!' "

The sermon which is spoken of as Whitefield's favorite sermon was on the text, "Behold the Lamb of God." This sermon has some expressions which would give offense today, even to those who are the most ardent believers in the substitutionary atonement; for example, where he speaks of Christ who "was thus roasted, as it were, in the Father's wrath, and therefore fitly styled the Lamb of God." Even Whitefield seems to have had doubt about that expression, since he inserts the clause "as it were"; but the sermon presents one great fact about the atonement that is today almost universally overlooked or left unspoken, namely, that the death of Christ on the cross was God's condemnation of sin, and that before the cross is a reconciliation, it is a condemnation, revealing the mind of God toward sin. It is only as a substitutionary death that the preaching of the death of Christ on the cross is used by the Holy Spirit to produce conversion.

The following sentences will give some suggestion of how Whitefield's description of the sufferings of Christ, the greatest theme which can engage the mind of a preacher, must have stirred him, and moved the thousands to whom he preached:

"If you can bear to be spectators of such an awful tragedy, as I desire you just now to go with me to the entrance, so I must entreat you to venture a little further into the same garden. But stop! What is it that we see? Behold the Lamb of God undergoing the most direful tortures of vindictive wrath! Of the people, of even his disciples, there is none with him. Alas! there was never sorrow like unto that sorrow wherewith his innocent soul was afflicted in this day of his Father's fierce anger.

"Before he entered into this bitter passion, out of the fullness of his heart he said, 'Now is my soul troubled.' But how is it troubled now? His agony bespeaks it to be exceeding sorrowful, even unto death. It extorts sweat, yea, a bloody sweat; his face, his hands, his garments, are all overstained with blood. It extorts strong crying and many tears. See how the incarnate Deity lies prostrate before his Father who now laid on him the iniquities of us all.

"See how he agonizes in prayer. Hark! again and again he addressed his Father with an 'If it be possible, let this cup pass from me.' Tell me, ye blessed angels, tell me, Gabriel, or whatsoever thou art called, who wast sent from heaven in this important hour to strengthen our agonizing Lord, tell me, if ye can, what Christ endured in this dark and doleful night, and tell me what you yourselves felt when you heard this same God-Man, whilst expiring on the accursed tree, breaking forth into that dolorous, unheard-of expostulation, 'My God, my God, why hast thou forsaken me?' Were you not all struck dumb, and did not a universal, awful silence fill heaven itself when God the Father said unto his sword, 'Sword, smite my fellow'?

"Well might nature put on its sable weeds; well might the rocks rend to show their sympathy with the suffering Saviour; and well might the sun withdraw its light as though it was shocked and confounded to see its Maker suffer. But our hearts are harder than rocks, otherwise they would now break, and our souls more stupid than any part of the inanimate creation, or they would even now in some degree at least sympathize with the crucified Redeemer."

This passage reminds one of William Wirt's beautiful description of the sacramental sermon of James Waddel, the famous blind preacher of Virginia.

Franklin wondered that the people resorted in such multitudes to hear themselves described as "half beasts and half devils." Whitefield did indeed declare in no uncertain tone the fall of man and the unregenerate state of man's heart, and therefore the necessity of regeneration, the new birth. But the secret of his power was not alone in the mere pronouncement of the great truths of the gospel, which every preacher ought to pronounce, and which the Holy Spirit honors in the conversion of souls, but also in the great love that Whitefield had for souls. When he saw the people he was moved with compassion. He used to speak of how he longed to roam the forests of America, "hunting for souls." That was his great quest, and whenever he preached men were made conscious of his love for their souls. "O Lord, grant me a warm heart!" was his frequent prayer.

This love for souls is what Wesley gives the first place in the account of Whitefield in his memorial sermon after his death: "He had a heart susceptible to the most generous and most tender friendship. I frequently thought that this, of all others, was the distinguishing part of his character. How few have we known of so kind a temper, of such large flowing affections! Was it not principally by this that the hearts of others were so strangely drawn and knit to him? Can anything but love beget love? This shone in his very countenance, and continually breathed in all his words, whether in public or private. It was the love of God shed abroad in his heart by the Holy Ghost which was given unto him, filling his soul with tender, disinterested love to every child of man. From this source arose that torrent of eloquence which frequently bore down all before it. From this that astonishing force of persuasion which the most hardened sinner could not resist. This it was which enabled him to pour out his soul in prayer in a manner peculiar to himself, with such fullness and ease united together, with such strength and variety both of sentiment and expression."

Whitefield was pre-eminently a *personal* preacher. In our day preaching has become too much the presentation of a proposition or a truth, and with too little of the personal appeal. But Whitefield constantly preached in the second person, and always it is "thou" and "you" that we hear. He was particularly effective, it was said, in the appeal at the conclusion of his sermon.

Whitefield was a great saint. He would not have been so great a preacher had it been otherwise. In a letter to the students at Harvard and Yale, who were zealous to carry on the great movement that had been started by Whitefield, he wrote this sentence, worthy of a place in every minister's study: "Henceforward, therefore, I hope you will enter into your studies, not to get a parish, nor to be polite preachers, but to be great saints."

James Harvey, one of the original Oxford Group, and one of Whitefield's converts, and author of *Meditations Among the Tombs*, said of Whitefield, "I never beheld so fair a copy of our Lord, such a divine image of the Saviour, or such exalted delight in God, such unbounded benevolences to man, such steady faith in the divine promises, such fervent zeal for the divine Glory."

Whitefield paid the price of sainthood. He gloried in the cross of Christ and gloried in the preaching of it, but he could also say, as Paul, "Whereby I am crucified unto the world and the world unto me." He lived near to God, and spent much time in prayer. Prayer, reading, and meditation, he said, were the chief preparations for preaching. And Whitefield was often and long at the golden altar of prayer. To a marked degree, also, Whitefield experienced joy in the divine friendship and companionship, and frequently we find him recording moments of ravishing and heavenly transport when he had met with God. His preaching never gave an outward demonstration that exceeded the inward reality. Like John the Baptist, he was a shining and burning light. He shone because he burned; and from the first sermon that he preached that day in St. Mary De Crypt down to the very end, the fire never sank and his love for Christ and his love for souls never grew cold.

His personal seal had for a device wings outspread for flight, and the motto it bore was, *"Astra petamus,"* "We desire the stars." And there among the stars we leave him; for "they that be wise shall shine as the brightness of the firmament; and they that turn many to righteousness as the stars for ever and ever."

MATTHEW SIMPSON

Matthew Simpson

IN THE Walnut Street Church of Chillicothe, Ohio, the reunion of the Ohio and Cincinnati Conferences of the Methodist Church was being celebrated. A member of the Conference, one of the editors of *The Christian Advocate*, was walking to the place of assembly with a friend. Bishop Simpson was to be the speaker. This man had never heard him speak, and said so to the friend with whom he was walking to the church. "He will draw you to your feet," said his friend. "I have been magnetized by him several times and compelled to get on my feet." "He will never do that with me," said the other. "I will keep my seat if the whole congregation gets up." But his friend said he would wait and see.

Coming early to the meeting, they selected a position from which they could see the whole audience. Bishop Simpson was delivering his famous speech on the future of the country. When he reached his first great climax, the audience rose to their feet in admiration and applause, but this man kept his seat as if he were an unmoved observer. Very soon all was quiet and calm again, and he congratulated himself that he had kept his word and won a victory. The others might rise and shout, but not he. After a little the bishop reached the second climax, mightier than the first, and again the whole audience arose with a great demonstration. This time the man had more difficulty in keeping his seat; but he remembered what he had said to his friend and was determined to sit still even if the roof of the building should fly off. He thought that the bishop had exhausted his oratorical resources and that from now on it would be no task to sit still. But presently Simpson reached his third and last climax, the famous passage in which he held aloft a battle-torn flag and began to apostrophize it. At this the great throng sprang again to their feet, and with them sprang up the man who was determined he would sit still though the roof of the building should fly off, shouting and cheering and weeping like the rest.

No one in the history of the American pulpit, and

no one indeed in the history of American oratory, seems to have had the power to get an audience to their feet like Bishop Matthew Simpson, the preacher of victorious faith and the greatest of the Methodists. Through a long ministry of more than fifty years Bishop Simpson demonstrated this singular power to magnetize an assemblage or congregation of human beings and lift them into transports of emotion and enthusiasm.

The last flash of that strange electric power was when he spoke on September 24, 1881, in Exeter Hall, London, at the memorial services for President Garfield. The meeting was presided over by James Russell Lowell, ambassador to Great Britain. Lowell made the opening address in beautiful and dignified speech. Then he called upon Bishop Simpson. Simpson was well acquainted with Garfield, as he had been with Lincoln, and could speak from the heart. After a touching reference to Garfield's mother, Simpson closed with these words: "I passed today the monuments of Wellington and Nelson, and it seemed to me that the heads of those heroes were bowed in grief. As I passed Westminster Abbey also, it seemed to me that the holy dead of past ages looked down with a greater solemnity and were waiting to be joined in that upper circle by the hero of the Western land." At this, although it was a solemn memorial service, a thing unheard of happened. The great audience sprang to their feet and applauded, and then sank down as quickly as they had risen up.

Men do not gather grapes of thorns, or figs of thistles. Wherever a great man, especially a great prophet or preacher, has arisen, you can count on it that the soil has been carefully prepared. Luke is careful to tell us that Zacharias and Elisabeth, the father and mother of John the Baptist, whom Christ declared was the greatest man who had ever lived, "were both righteous before God." Out of such a God-fearing and intelligent family came this great preacher. He had an uncle, too, a man of noble parts, who prayed for him every day, and was wont to say to him, "Remember, you are a child of Providence." His family were Scotch-Irish Presbyterians who had come under the spell of John Wesley. They had migrated to America and settled at Cadiz, Ohio, where Simpson was born June 21, 1811. He was educated at the Cadiz Academy and spent a brief period at Madison College, a Methodist college then located at Uniontown, Pennsylvania. There he came under the spell of some of the great Methodist preachers. When he returned to Cadiz he took up the study of medicine, qualified himself as a practitioner, accumulated some books and instruments, and commenced the work of his profession. But God had chosen him as a physican for souls.

Always devout and prayerful, through his godly training and environment kept from gross transgression, he had not yet made a profession of his faith in Christ. But one evening, standing near the railing of the altar at a camp meeting, although he himself was not stirred, he laid his hand on the shoulder of a young man in whom he was interested and asked him if he would like to go forward for prayer. The young man answered that he would go if Simpson would go with him, and together they went to the altar and knelt down. It was after this that Simpson made a profession of his faith and united with the Church. He had good prospects as a physician, but the hand of God was on him for the ministry. At a night meeting his godly uncle said to him, "Don't you think you could speak to the people tonight?" That night he made his first Christian address, and immediately men marked his ability. One thing that held him back from a decision for the ministry was the fact that he was the only son of a widowed mother and could not bear the thought of leaving her. But one day he ventured to introduce the subject to his mother. With a smile on her face and tears in her eyes, his rejoicing mother said, "My son, I have been looking for this hour ever since you were born." Simpson used to relate this incident with great effect when he was at the height of his fame as a minister.

He received an appointment on the St. Clairsville circuit in Ohio, and preached his first sermon at New Athens, on John 12:35, "Walk while ye have the light." When at St. Clairsville he was tempted to give up the ministry because of the discouragement he felt after hearing a sermon by a very able preacher; but not long afterward he heard a very poor sermon by a very poor preacher, and this determined him to stick to his pulpit until a better man should appear. His next appointment was to the Pittsburgh Circuit, where he became an assistant, or rotating, preacher at the Smithfield Methodist Church, and also at the Liberty Street Methodist Church, where for a time he was also the regular preacher. In 1836 he was appointed to Williamsport, now Monongahela City. At this time he drew up his plan of life and work, to which he earnestly adhered in the years to come. This is the way he put it: "First, what I should refrain from: Never injure the feelings of any person with whom I converse or am associated. Speak evil of no one. Suffer not myself to give way to jesting or jocose spirits. Second, what I should do: Rise at four every morning, and if I cannot retire at a corresponding hour, sleep a sufficient time to make up the deficiency during the day. Devote some time to the Scriptures in their original. Reprove sin wherever I find it. If commended, pray for humility. If insulted, pray for love. If apparently successful, be thankful to God and pray to feel my own unworthiness. To preach, exhort, and pray as though in the immediate presence of Jehovah himself."

In 1837, Simpson was elected to the chair of natural science at Allegheny College at Meadville, recently taken over from the Presbyterians. After two years at Allegheny College, he became president of Asbury University at Greencastle, Indiana, afterward DePauw University. Simpson threw himself into the work of building up this university and building up Methodism with great enthusiasm. At his first commencement he had for one of his speakers Henry Ward Beecher, then a young minis-

ter in the Second Presbyterian Church of Indianapolis. The two young men within twenty-five
years were destined to be the most famous preachers
in America. Simpson constantly rode the circuit in
Indiana, for that state was then a wilderness. In a
real sense, therefore, he belongs to the heroic order
of the circuit-riding preachers, most illustrious of
whom were Francis Asbury and Peter Cartwright.
This was a great training school: "Her academic
groves are the boundless forests and prairies of these
western wilds. Her Acadian groves and orchard
songs are the wild woods and the birds of every
color and every note, relieved now and then by the
bass hooting of the owl and the weird trilling of
the whippoorwill. Her curricula are the philosophies
of nature and the mysteries of redemption. Her li-
brary is the Word of God, the Discipline, and the
Hymn Book, supplemented by trees and brooks and
stones, all of which are full of wisdom and sermons
and speeches; and her parchment of literary honors
are the horse and saddlebags." From this circuit-
riding experience Simpson drew some of his most
telling illustrations in his sermons of the future.

In 1844 he was a delegate to the General Conference which met in New York, where he listened

to the great debates over the question of slavery that resulted in the disruption of the Methodist Church. In 1848 he became the editor of the *Western Christian Advocate*, where his powerful editorials on the subject of slavery secured him the acquaintance and friendship of the foremost defender of the fugitive slave and the great organizer of antislavery societies and parties, Salmon P. Chase, afterward Lincoln's Secretary of the Treasury. In 1852 he was elected a bishop of the Methodist Church, and took up his residence in Pittsburgh, where he resided until he moved to Evanston, Illinois, in 1859.

When the storm of the Civil War broke over the country, Simpson had his great opportunity as an oracle of the people. He encouraged the soul of the nation and strengthened its hand in the Lord. He was one of Lincoln's most welcome friends and advisers. Simpson relates how on one occasion he and Lincoln prayed around twice on the subject of emancipation. The gruff and severe Stanton, when Simpson called, would leave the crowd in his outside office and, leading the bishop into a private room, would often say to him, "Now, Bishop, pray."

During the war, Simpson was the evangelist of patriotism and the chief pulpit voice in America.

In most of the cities of the North he delivered his famous lecture on the future of our country. The delivery of this lecture stirred great enthusiasm in the audiences which listened to it. Men would shout, laugh, cry, throw their hats in the air, and beat one another on the back under the spell of the bishop's speech. It was in this address that, holding a battle-torn flag in his hand, he would refer to the flag as: "Some patch of that azure filled with stars that an angel has snatched from the heavenly canopy to set the stripes in blood. . . . The blood of our brave boys is upon it, the bullets of rebels have gone through and through it, yet it is the same old flag. Our fathers followed that flag. We expect that our children and our children's children will follow it. There is nothing on earth like that old flag for beauty. Long may these stars shine! Just now there are clouds upon it, and mists are gathering around it. But the stars are coming out, and others are joining them, and they grow brighter and brighter, and so may they shine till the last star in the heavens shall fall!"

When Lincoln was laid low by the assassin's bullet, Simpson was summoned to the White House, where he made the prayer at the funeral. By common consent he, and not Henry Ward Beecher or any of the political orators and leaders of the day, was selected to express the nation's thought of Lincoln at the final services at Springfield, Illinois. Standing on the oak-covered hillside on that bright May morning in 1865, Simpson delivered a noble eulogy. In this oration Simpson revealed the fact that Lincoln had frequently said to him: "I never shall live out the four years of my term. When the rebellion is crushed, my work is done." In the concluding paragraph Simpson said: "Chieftain, farewell! The nation mourns thee. Mothers shall teach thy name to their lisping children. The youth of our land shall emulate thy virtues. Statesmen shall study thy record, and from it learn lessons of wisdom. Mute though thy lips be, yet they still speak. Hushed is thy voice, but its echoes of liberty are ringing through the world, and the sons of bondage listen with joy. Thou didst not fall for thyself. The assassin had no hate for thee. Our hearts were aimed at; our national life was sought. We crown thee as our martyr, and humanity enthrones thee as her triumphant son. Hero, martyr, friend, farewell!"

Simpson's preaching, as well as his public addresses, aroused almost unbelievable enthusiasm in his hearers. It was well known that the loud and fervent shouting which characterized the Methodist assemblies of that day somewhat disturbed him when he was preaching, and it was not an unusual sight to see men sitting in the pews with clenched hands, striving to hold back the emotion within them that was struggling for utterance. Two ministers went to hear him preach his famous sermon on "Ezekiel's Vision of the Holy Waters." As he described the growth and spread of the sacred stream, first water to the ankles, and then to the knees, then to the loins, and then a river to swim in, every new advance was marked with tears and shouting by the congregation. One of the two ministers held the knees of the other so as to keep him from stamping, and finally, to keep him from shouting, forced his head down between the seats. One who heard Simpson preach his sermon on "Enoch" relates how the climax of the sermon was a description of the first redeemed sinner's arrival in heaven. The gates stood ajar and the ranks of the angels parted, that this one sinner, washed in the blood of Christ, might pass on up to the throne. The audience was swept with emotion as the sinner was seen going up to the throne. At this a minister of towering form and stentorian voice cried out in his ecstasy: "Amen! Let him go!"

From the time that he first commenced to preach as a young man in Pittsburgh, Bishop Simpson determined to be an extemporaneous preacher in the real sense of the word. He kept a commonplace book in which he jotted down texts that appealed to him; but he wrote nothing, save a skeleton page perhaps a few hours before the time for preaching, which he never took with him into the pulpit. Thus he developed a readiness of speech which characterized his public utterance. Yet his sermons were always thoughtful. Spurgeon told his American friends that he followed the same plan. Saturday afternoon he would select the text and make an outline. He would do the same before the time for the second sermon. This seems almost unbelievable, when we consider the orderly nature of his discourses. Beecher worked along the same general lines. We can understand the success of it more easily in his case, for Beecher was a spontaneous, explosive genius, who drew his lightning from the sky.

Very early in his career Simpson broke the bondage of the idea that a sermon must not be repeated. Like Chalmers he repeated his sermons over and over again, and when he came to address conferences and other religious gatherings there were certain sermons that people asked for, and it was expected that he would preach them. He was always deeply in earnest. One who as a young minister had him come to preach for him in his own small frame church to a little group of people, said that he preached one of his famous sermons and with the same earnestness with which he preached it to thousands at the camp meetings.

It were vain to attempt to analyze the secret of Bishop Simpson's power over an audience. One might as well attempt to analyze the sunrise, or the light of a star. But the man's message is no secret. He trod the broad territory of the great cardinal doctrines of the Christian faith. When Charles Francis Adams, our ambassador to England during the Civil War, heard Spurgeon preach in his tabernacle, this was the impression he noted down: "There was no characteristic thought or novel reasoning. His power consisted in sympathy with the current of human feeling in all ages on that solemn topic of moral responsibility to a higher power, both here and hereafter." So was the preaching of Simpson. He struck the major chords of the human heart and dealt with the accepted truths of the Christian faith. I call him the "Preacher of Victorious Faith," not only because that was the subject of his most famous sermon, "The Victory of Faith," I John 5:4, but because he was a preacher who in all his sermons dwelt upon the "exceeding greatness" of the Christian revelation and its power to give man victory over all his enemies in this life and to bestow upon him a glorious immortality in the life which is to come. The two great notes in his preaching, I should say, were the victory of faith in this world and the reward of faith in the world which is to come. Simpson believed in heaven, delighted himself in the prospect of sharing its great joys, and summoned others to a like expectation.

Here are a few examples of how he blended this great music, the triumph of faith in this life and its reward in the life to come. In his sermon on "The Victory of Faith," he gives this fine illustration of how faith holds a man steady in this life: "The old men of this country were often called to pass swollen streams before bridges were built. Mounted on the backs of strong horses, they plunged fearlessly in. If they looked upon the rapid flow of the waters, their brains grew unsteady. They seemed to be carried against the current and were in danger of falling off and being drowned. But if they raised their eyes and looked at some tree top or some hill top beyond, or at some rock that jutted from the shore, they passed safely and quietly over. It was the view of the distant that steadied them against the whirl of the present." In the conclusion of this sermon, Simpson lets himself go in a flight of noble imagination. He first describes the genius of infidelity, conducting him through the earth, showing him the beauties and splendors of the world, the rocks and fossils and their stories of ancient catastrophes. Then the genius of infidelity conducts him into the heavens and shows him the solar system and goes with him from world to world until they have reached the last star in the suburbs of the universe. There he sits down and, looking up into the face of his guide, asks, "Is this all?" Surprised at this, the genius of infidelity asks if it is not enough—enough and so wonderful as to occupy all his thought and fill all his heart? But there is still a void within his soul. The genius of infidelity then leaves him and the genius of Christianity comes to his side. She conducts him through the same worlds, shows him the same wonders in heaven above, on the earth beneath, and in

70

the waters under the earth. When they have reached the last star he gazes into the face of his guide and asks again, "Is this all?" With a look of pity and yet of love, his guide exclaims: "Is this all! This is but the portico; it is the entrance to the Father's house." And she puts the glass of faith in my hand, and I look through it, and away beyond the stars, away beyond the multiplied systems, I see the great center, the throne of God, about which all things move, the great central point of the universe; and as I look, there is One upon the throne. He is my Brother, and I look again, and my name is written on his hands, and I cry out with ecstasy,

"Before the throne my Surety stands;
My name is written on his hands."

A characteristic sermon by Simpson on this subject of the power of faith here and hereafter is the one on "The Power of the Invisible," on the text, "We look not at the things which are seen," II Cor. 4:18. His proposition is how by the religious concentration of thought on the life to come it is made real to us, not by an occasional glance, but by the steady gaze and concentration. The benefit of such contemplation is that it gives us stability amid the storms and uncertainties of this life. In the old days men who sailed the seas steered by the objects they saw on the land; but when the compass was discovered and its needle pointed always toward the north, then the sailor was able to keep steadily on his way without regard for the things near him or around him. So is it in life. Man needs faith in the unseen in order that he may be strong and courageous in the midst of the present world.

The preacher is not afraid to look into eternity and never doubts that the future life will be better than this life. On the always timely topic of recognition of our friends in heaven, Simpson uses rather unusual illustrations or Scriptural proofs. First, he speaks of the daughter of Jairus, who was dead and brought back to life by our Lord: "She had been dead. And now let me ask this question: Do you suppose that damsel when she came to life again recognized her mother? Did she know her father? She had died. And if death destroys memory, her memory was gone. If death destroys associations, her associations of thought were gone. And had she come back again without memory, without the strength of association, and without attachment to her friends, what would life have been? But, methinks, when she opened her eyes she threw her arms around her mother's neck."

In the same striking way the great preacher makes use of the restoration of the widow's son, the resurrection of Lazarus, and the appearance of Moses and Elijah on the mount. Then he breaks into this noble passage: "Oh, they do care about earth! They do come back to earth! The glorified saints love our earth still. . . . Our kindred in heaven love us still. The mother who counseled me and bore me when an infant, who talked to me in my riper years, and whom I laid in the grave a few months ago, she is my mother still. Beyond the dark curtain which hides immortality from view, she is the same still. She loves me still. If I but give my heart to God, and discharge my duty, she waits to welcome me in the spirit world. The song of joy is going up just on the other side. Methinks white hands are beckoning to some of us. A little longer bear earth's jars and toils, and then go up higher. The invisible is flaming in light; and as I look out, it becomes a joy to my heart."

Simpson has a notable sermon on Stephen, in which he strikes the chord of the future life, and much besides. His chief points in this sermon are:

73

First, that Stephen exercised himself in Christian service and testimony, and that exercise is the law of growth. He well says, "The reason why very many have not the spirit of the Lord Jesus, and are not abundant in the consolation of the gospel, is that they will not do the work of Christ." His second point is that when a man makes an earnest effort, as Stephen did in behalf of the cause of God, he can stand unmoved in the midst of his enemies. The third point, and the most important, is that fidelity to God brings a vision of heaven and of Christ. He emphasizes the fact seldom, perhaps never, spoken of, that the death of Stephen was not only the death of the first martyr but the first Christian death recorded. He imagines what the first disciples must have thought about dying, and how death and its great change would strike them in their new belief. "Perhaps," he says, "they thought they must die in agony as Jesus did, and with a sense of having been forsaken. But the death of Stephen, with its vision of the glory of Christ, was the answer to their wonder."

Stephen saw heaven opened "and Jesus standing on the right hand of God." If men are to see the heavenly light and to see Christ in glory, then their hearts must be free of enmity toward any child of man. This was so in the case of Stephen, for when he was dying he prayed, "Lord, lay not this sin to their charge."

After mentioning several cases where the departing soul was granted a rapture in death, Simpson acknowledges that the eye of the dying man can see no farther, and his ear hear no more, than the eyes and ears of those who stand about him. But there is the seeing of the soul and the hearing of the soul. The man who walks with God and trusts in Christ will see heaven opened as truly as Stephen did. The great question, then, is, Are we ready to die? "Live for Him, and all will be well in the dying hour. Live for Jesus and he will never forget you. If you live for fame, men may turn against you. If you live for pleasure, your ability to enjoy it may pass away and your senses grow dim. If you live for the mazy dance, your feet may be unable to move. If you live for the beautiful, your sense of sight may fail you. If you live for your children, they may be smitten down and leave you desolate; or, what is far worse, they may desert you and leave you worse than childless in a cold and unfeeling world. If you live for any joy of earth, you may be forsaken; but, oh, live for Jesus, and he will never forsake you!"

In a noble sermon on posthumous influence, "He

Being Dead Yet Speaketh," Simpson describes the influence of the Christian life and how true glory comes from serving God. Abel fell, and to human eyes his life was ended, and yet, "he being dead yet speaketh." "He speaks in his fidelity to truth, for he was the first martyr to the truth. There were angels in heaven before, and archangels, seraph and cherub, were there. There was the song of created praise in heaven before; but there never was a human soul. I do not know when the last addition will be made to heaven's intellectual forces. I know not when archangels and angels and seraph and cherub received their birth. I know not whether for ages there had been one addition to heaven's choir. There had been angels who lost their place, whose thrones were vacant because they disobeyed; but I know of no fresh gathering into the realm of glory until Abel led the way. And then, too, Abel's advent to heaven marked a new era in the universe. It was not merely the ascent of a human soul; it was the striking of the note of the new song. The angels' voices had been singing creation's praise from creation's morn, when the morning stars sang together, and all the sons of God shouted for joy; but when this spirit rose from earth, when Abel ascended, it was not of creation that he sang. He struck a new note, and as he sang it was, Unto him that loved me and washed me from my sins in his own blood and made me a king and a priest unto God; unto him be glory and power and dominion forever and forever. But the ages rolled on, and others came. The choir has been increasing all the time. The songs have been sounding. The glory fills heaven. 'T is more than heaven can contain, for the angels who have listened to that song for the hundreds of years were so charmed by it that when heaven's doors were opened, they came down to try to sing some of the same notes in shepherds' ears, and said, 'Glory to God in the highest, peace on earth, good will to men.' Abel had told of a Saviour. Then angels came to sing him born.

"The song is growing. Heaven is happier every day. There is now more music, more power, more joy in heaven than there has ever been before. I love music. I love the tones that thrill the soul, though God has given me but little power to sing. I delight in the music of earth. I think I shall delight far more in the music of heaven, and I sometimes fancy that though I cannot sing much here, I shall sing there. At least I shall try to strike the note that has been running through heaven so long, and when it comes to the word 'me' I shall try to say it: 'Loved me, washed me in His own blood. Loved me, and made me a king and priest unto God. Unto him be glory forever and forever!' "

One who heard Simpson preach this sermon on the victory of faith before a New England congregation thus describes his appearance and action: "His height and gently stooping figure suggested a kind of scholarly awkwardness. His features pale, strongly and sharply cut, but by no means classic in their mold, intimated a certain strength of character, but nothing more. The eyelids drooped slightly over the sad, almost expressionless, leaden-blue eyes, deeply sunken under his broad, low brow, which was surmounted by thin, slight, straight light-brown hair, slightly tinged with gray. The voice began in a thin, husky, nasal, high-pitched, and an almost feeble tone. The words were slowly, but clearly, enunciated. There was little in the appearance of the man to indicate the treasure within. For the first fifteen minutes a stranger would be likely to experience a sense of disappointment. But the eagle was only reserving its strength for an upward flight. As he gradually worked himself into the heart of his subject, as feeling gathered, his quavering tenor voice grew penetrating, resonant, sympathetic, and impassioned. The stooping figure became erect, the dull eyes were kindled into a blaze by the long-pent-up fire within. His thoughts seemed to play over his face like a luminously radiating atmosphere. The sentences grew short and pithy, and were uttered with an incisiveness and a rapidity of enunciation and a peculiar stress of voice upon the final words. Whenever he touched the finer chords of feeling, there was a thrilling melody in his tones like the native music of the land of his Irish ancestors, full of plaintiveness, with now and then a kind of wailing tenderness of pathos."

The one who gives this account of the preacher says that at the close hundreds shouted, clapped their hands, rose to their feet, and men and women wept and laughed at once as they gazed upon the vision of their inheritance with the saints in light. The inheritance is just as great for the believer to-day as in the past ages of faith.

Nearly all reports of the preaching of Bishop Simpson indicate that at the beginning of his sermon or address his speech was ordinary, commonplace, and a disappointment to the hearer. The following is the record of one who heard him during the Civil War, when he was at the height of his fame and made one of his most famous addresses:

"In 1863, walking the streets of Philadelphia one night with an army surgeon, we passed the Academy of Music in that city, where a meeting was being held on behalf of the Christian Commission, the object of which was to take care of wounded soldiers. As we stood at the back of the stage listening, the meeting seemed to be very dull. A speaker was introduced. His voice was thin, his manner unimpressive. My friend said, 'Let's go,' but I replied, 'Wait until we see what there is in him.' Suddenly he grew upon us. The address became adorned with a pathos, a sublimity, and an enthusiasm that overwhelmed the audience. When the speaker sat down, I inquired who he was.

" 'That is Bishop Simpson,' said my informant. In later years I learned that the bishop's address that night was the great hour of his life. His reputation became national. He was one of the few old men who knew how to treat young men. He used no gestures on the platform, no climaxes, no dramatic effects of voice, yet he was eloquent beyond description. His earnestness broke over and broke through all rules of rhetoric. He made his audiences think and feel as he did himself. That, I believe, is the best of a man's inner salvation."

The secret of the sway of Simpson, so far as any such secret can be told, lay in the fact that people like to have their hearts warmed, and that when they came to hear him preach he warmed their hearts. Always there was a fervor in his preaching, and always there was the deep earnestness of one who would preach "as a dying man to dying men." This was the standard that Simpson set for the preacher in his Yale Lectures on Preaching: "The minister should never forget that preaching is designed for immediate effect. So far as the mere thought is concerned, a book is better for study than a sermon. The living preacher is with the word to give it immediate force. His message is, 'Now is the accepted time; behold, now is the day of salvation.' Whenever he preaches with the fancy that his sermons will do good sometime next year, he widely misses the mark. They are forgotten almost as soon as delivered. It is the present impression for which sermons are preached. Ever remember that God sends people to hear, as well as you to preach; that your sermon may be the last one which some poor sinner may hear before he is summoned to the bar of God.

Say something which the poor soldier on the battle-field, whose life blood is oozing away, or a culprit on the gallows, would wish to hear before dropping into eternity."

Not until we have another Civil War, with the tremendous passions which were aroused, will the stage be set for popular preachers like the two great preachers of that epoch, Beecher and Simpson. But the human soul remains the same from age to age. Life still has its woes and the heart its sorrows and its passions. Man is the same, and Christ is the same "yesterday, and to day, and for ever." There is a great age of preaching to come, as well as in the past. When the great revival which the country and the Church so sorely need begins to blow over the land, that revival will have great heralds and voices, reasoning with men of righteousness and temperance and judgment to come, and describing for them in terms of burning eloquence the glory of the inheritance of the saints. Then again men will bow before the spell of the preacher, and again they shall say, "How beautiful upon the mountains are the feet of him that bringeth good tidings, that publisheth peace; that bringeth good tidings of good, that publisheth salvation; that saith unto Zion, Thy God reigneth!"

HENRY WARD BEECHER

Henry Ward Beecher

HENRY WARD BEECHER was a great son of a
great father. Lyman Beecher, his father, was perhaps
the greatest preacher of his day and generation in
America. His sermon preached after the duel between Aaron Burr and Alexander Hamilton, and
the series of sermons on intemperance, preached at
Litchfield, Connecticut, in 1814, rank among the
most powerful utterances in the history of the American pulpit. After pastorates at East Hampton, Long
Island; Litchfield, Connecticut; and Boston, Lyman
Beecher, in 1832, became president of the newly
established Lane Theological Seminary of the Presbyterian Church at Cincinnati. At the time of the
schism in the Presbyterian Church between the Old
and New Schools, he was tried for heresy by the

Presbytery of Cincinnati, but was acquitted. John Todd said of him: "Lyman Beecher was a thunderbolt. You never knew where it would strike. But you never saw him rise to speak without feeling that so much electricity must strike."

Henry Ward Beecher was born June 24, 1813, in Litchfield, Connecticut. He was the eighth child of the remarkable Beecher family, one of whom was Harriet Beecher Stowe, author of the *Minister's Wooing, Dred,* and *Uncle Tom's Cabin.* So distinguished was this Beecher family that someone spoke of dividing humanity into three parts—"the good, the bad, and the Beechers." Henry Ward Beecher's mother, Roxanna Foote, "was a shy, sensitive, self-abnegating woman, who loved flowers and all beautiful things, sang, played the guitar, did fine embroidery, and painted on ivory." She died when Henry was only three years of age. Beecher afterward wrote of his mother, "If I were asked what had been in my own ministry the unseen source of more help and more power than anything else, I should say that my mother gave to me a temperament that enabled me to see the unseeable and to know the unknowable, to realize things not created as if they were, and oftentimes far more than if they were, present to my outward senses."

As a lad Henry determined to go to sea, but his father persuaded him that he must first learn navigation, so he was sent to the Mt. Pleasant Institute at Amherst. In 1830 he entered Amherst College, where he distinguished himself as an orator. Because of a defect in his verbal memory, his teachers in the primary schools had regarded him as unusually stupid. After graduating from Amherst he entered the Lane Theological Seminary at Cincinnati, of which his father was the head. There he sang in the choir of the Church of the Covenant, where his father preached; conducted a Bible class; gave temperance lectures; and preached on Sundays when he had opportunity. When in the seminary he was a witness of the riots when the printing press of James G. Birney, editor of an antislavery paper, was destroyed.

He had made a confession of his faith when a lad and joined his father's church in Boston. But his real spiritual experience came while he was a student in the seminary. He speaks of a beautiful May morning in the Ohio woods, "when it pleased God to reveal to my wandering soul the idea that it was his nature to love a man in his sins for the sake of helping him out of them. . . . And when I found that Jesus Christ had such a disposition, I felt that

I had found a God. I shall never forget the feelings with which I walked forth that May morning. The golden pavements will never feel to my feet as then the grass felt to them; and the singing of the birds in the woods—for I roamed in the woods—was cacophonous to the sweet music of my thoughts; and there were no forms in the universe which seemed to me graceful enough to represent the Being, a conception of whose character had just dawned on my mind. I felt when I had with the psalmist called upon the heavens, the earth, the mountains, the streams, the floods, the birds, the beasts, and universal being, to praise God, that I had called upon nothing that could praise him enough for the revelation of such a nature as that in the Lord Jesus Christ."

This was the beautiful spiritual experience upon which Henry Ward Beecher drew all through the years of his notable ministry. Ofttimes inconsistent and illogical, and sometimes seeming to assail cardinal Christian truth, he had always a deep love for man and a great love for Christ, and a passion to make men Christlike.

His first church was at Lawrenceburgh, Indiana, on the Ohio River, twenty miles south of Cincinnati. Beecher thus describes his first congregation:

"The flock which I found gathered in the wilderness consisted of twenty persons: nineteen of them were women, and the other was nothing. I was sexton of my own church at that time. There were no lamps there, so I bought some and I filled them and lighted them. I swept the church, and lighted my own fire. I did not ring the bell because there was none to ring. I opened the church before prayer meeting and meeting, and locked it when they were over."

On August 3, 1837, Beecher married Eunice Bullard, of West Sutton, Massachusetts, to whom he had become engaged when a student at Amherst. The couple went to housekeeping over a stable, and so straitened were their circumstances with an annual salary of $300 that Beecher was glad to accept castoff clothing from others. He would not pledge adhesion to the Old School Presbyterian General Assembly, and was refused ordination by the Miami Presbytery. His church supported him in his stand and became an independent church. Beecher was afterward ordained by the New School Presbytery of Cincinnati.

In 1839 he became pastor of the Second Presbyterian Church of Indianapolis. Indianapolis was then a rough frontier town. The railroad was yet twenty miles distant from the capital. During these eight years in Indianapolis Beecher established an early fame as a popular preacher. His church was soon crowded. The people liked his unconventional ways. He is said to have been one of the first ministers to appear in public wearing a soft hat. Also he tried his hand as an editor, taking charge of a department of the *Western Farmer and Gardener*. Frequently he would be seen painting his house, carrying a hose to a town fire, or wheeling his groceries home in a wheelbarrow. It was during these years that he preached his celebrated sermons dealing with the vices of the frontier community, such as "Twelve Causes of Dishonesty," "Gamblers and Gambling," and "The Strange Woman." These were afterward published under the title "Twelve Lectures to Young Men" and were widely read throughout the country. Beecher says that the lectures were delivered on successive Sunday nights, and that the church was crowded during the series, "a thing that seldom happened during my Western life."

Here is a sample of these sermons, a paragraph from the one on the text, "My Son, If Sinners Entice Thee, Consent Thou Not." After describing the tempter who defiles the youth and seduces him to evil, the preacher says, "Had I a son of years, I could with thanksgiving see him go down to the grave rather than to fall into the maw of this most besotted devil. The plague is merciful, the cholera is love, the deadliest fever is refreshment to man's body in comparison with this epitome and essence of moral disease. He lives among men, Hell's ambassador, with full credentials, nor can we conceive that there should be need of any other fiend to perfect the works of darkness while he carries his body among us, stuffed with every pestilent drug of corruption. The heart of every virtuous young man should loathe him; if he speaks you should as soon hear a wolf bark. Gather around you the venomous snake, the poisonous toad, the fetid vulture, the prowling hyena, and their company would be an honor to you above his, for they at least remain within their own nature, but he goes out of his nature so that he becomes more vile than it is possible for a mere animal to be."

The sermon on "Gamblers and Gambling," based on the incident of the soldiers gambling at the cross for the garments of Jesus, pictures four scenes: The first is a genteel coffeehouse, where the youth sips his wine and deals his cards. The second scene shows a silent room, where four men sit motionless save as to their hands about the gaming table. One of the four, and the fiercest of them, is the young man from the coffeehouse, who sat down somewhat reluctantly just to make out a game with the others. The third scene shows a dirty room and a dilapidated house near the landing in New Orleans. In this den is a dropsical wretch, vermin-covered and stenchful; a scoundrel Spaniard; a burly Negro and drunken sailors; and "ogling, thieving, drinking women, who should have died long ago when all that was womanly died." Then comes the rough-and-tumble fight between the gamblers, the worst of whom is the once undefiled young man who started by an innocent game in the coffeehouse. Then comes the fourth and last scene: A cart drags a thrice-guarded wretch to the gallows. "At the gallows ladder his courage fails, his coward feet refuse to ascend. Dragged up, he is supported by bustling officials. His brain reels, his eye swims, while the meek minister utters a final prayer by his leaden ear. The prayer is said, the noose is fixed, the signal is given, a shudder runs through the crowd as he swings free. After a moment his convulsed limbs stretch down and hang heavily and still, and he who began to gamble to make up a game, and ended with stabbing an enraged victim whom he had fleeced, has here played his last game, himself the stake."

In the sermon on "The Strange Woman" is this fine passage: "The heart of youth is a wide prairie. Over it hang the clouds of heaven to water it. The sun throws its broad sheets of light upon it to wake its life. Out of its bosom spring, the long season through, flowers of a hundred names and hues, twining together their lovely forms, wafting to each other a grateful odor, and nodding each to each in summer breeze. Oh, such would man be did he hold that purity of heart which God gave him! But you have a depraved heart. It is a vast continent. On it are mountain ranges of power, and dark, deep streams, and pools and morasses. If once the full and terrible clouds of temptation do settle thick and fixedly upon you, and begin to cast down their dreadful stores, may God save man whom man can never."

It was not strange that a preacher who could paint scenes like these was soon heard of outside of Indianapolis. In 1847, after he had declined calls to the Park Street Church of Boston and the Old South

Church of Boston, he accepted a call to the newly
organized Plymouth Church of Brooklyn. A few
earnest men, Congregationalists, who were interested in civic righteousness and religious liberty, had
purchased an abandoned Presbyterian Church and
asked Beecher to become their minister. Something
about this call appealed to Beecher and on October
10, 1847, he commenced his ministry of forty years
in Brooklyn. During the first months his preaching
attracted little attention, but after a time the church
was too small for the congregations. This gave
Beecher an opportunity to have a church built in
accordance with his own ideas. The result was the
famous Plymouth Church, seating, when crowded,
about two thousand five hundred people. It was a
plain, unadorned building, but one which brought
the congregation near to the preacher and with excellent acoustics. Everyone could see the preacher
and the preacher could see everyone in his congregation. Beecher would never have a pulpit. In his Yale
Lectures he spoke of the importance of the projec-
tion of the minister's personality to the congregation. Among the chief hindrances to this, he claimed,
was the separation of the pews from the pulpit by a
great space between the two. Another was the "barrel

pulpit." "I think the matter so important," he said, "that I tell the truth and lie not when I say that I would not accept a settlement in a very advantageous place if I was obliged to preach out of one of those old-fashioned swallows' nests on the wall."

Beecher believed that a preacher should preach with his whole body. "A man's whole form is a part of his public speaking, his feet speak and so do his hands. You put a man in one of these barrel pulpits where there is no responsibility laid upon him as to his body and he falls into all manner of gawky attitudes and rests himself like a country horse at a hitching post."

Beecher claimed that the gap between the ordinary pulpit and the people was like a Sahara Desert, and before a man can fill such a space his magnetic influence is all lost. Preaching with a gap between the pulpit and the people he spoke of "as though a man should sit on one side of a river and try to win a mistress on the other side, bawling out his love at the top of his voice. However she might have been inclined, one such shout would be too much for tender sentiments."

The congregation was intelligent, middle-class people, not wealthy, ready for a new voice and giving complete freedom to the preacher. Every year the pews were auctioned off, and before the time set for the auctioning of the pews, it was the custom of Beecher to preach a sermon setting forth his views on religious and social questions. In this way he was able to secure a congregation who supported him in all for which he stood. One of the features of the worship at Plymouth Church was the hearty congregational singing. To develop this, Beecher prepared the well-known *Plymouth Collection*, with hymns and tunes gathered from all sources, something of an innovation at that time.

Beecher had a high purpose when he came to Brooklyn to make Plymouth 'Church a spiritual church. His early ministry was marked by a series of revivals. In 1857 one of the members of his church started a Monday morning prayer meeting. At first Beecher would have nothing to do with it. Later on, he always presided. Some who heard Beecher often have said that he was at his best in these informal prayer-meeting talks, at which he always sat. Beecher's power as a revivalist was as a preacher of the love of God. Perhaps he did not do justice to the law, to sin, and the sterner side of the Christian revelation, but he knew how to draw men with the bands of love.

He once said of the great evangelist Finney, "I have sat in my own pulpit and seen Finney get the sinner down and pound him until I have wanted to pull Finney by the coat and cry out: 'Oh, let him up! Let him up.'" That was the great Finney's method. He drove men to repentance, whereas Beecher drew them.

The agitation about slavery was stirring the country when Beecher went to Brooklyn. During his ministry in Indianapolis, he had little to say upon this dangerous theme, but in Brooklyn he made his platform a sounding board for the antislavery cause. One of the dramatic incidents in this connection was when at the Broadway Tabernacle in New York he auctioned off two young Negresses of light complexion, who, finding they were about to be sold from Washington to a slave dealer at New Orleans, had attempted to escape and had been brought back to Washington. At the public meeting held in the Broadway Tabernacle in their interests, Beecher called for bids, and the money necessary to set them free was quickly raised. This was the first of a series of mock slave auctions carried on by Beecher during the years before the outbreak of the Civil War.

As one of the editors of *The Independent,*

Beecher wrote editorials which were widely read and had great influence throughout the country wherever slavery was discussed. It was after Webster had espoused Henry Clay's compromise measure in his famous seventh-of-March speech in 1850, that Beecher made the celebrated allusion to Webster as "Lucifer fallen from heaven": "I cannot but cry out in the deepest sorrow, 'O Lucifer, son of the morning, how art thou fallen!' I would not speak harshly of Daniel Webster. The time was when there was no man I so much revered and for statesman's genius, for stature of understanding, there is no man on the globe since the death of Robert Peel, who is his equal. No; I would not cast stones at him. I would rather do as the sons of Noah, and going backward, cast a cloak over his nakedness."

In 1856, Beecher took the stump for John C. Fremont, the first candidate of the newly formed Republican Party. One of the charges against Fremont was that he was a Roman Catholic. This charge was false and was based on the fact that in his runaway marriage to Jessie Benton, the ceremony had been performed by a Catholic priest. Beecher made the charge ridiculous with his story of the dog Noble at the empty hole. He told of a dog which had seen a red squirrel once run into a hole in a stone wall, and could never be persuaded that he was not there forever. "When all other occupations failed this hole remained to him. When there were no chickens to harry, no pigs to bite, no cattle to chase, no children to romp with, no expeditions to make with the grown folks, and when he had slept all that his dog skin would hold, he would go out of the yard, yawn, and stretch himself, and then look wistfully at the hole, as if thinking to himself, 'Well, as there is nothing else to do, I may as well try that hole again.' "

Beecher took an active part in the successful Lincoln campaign of 1860. After Lincoln's election a mob hurled stones through the windows of his church and he had to be escorted home by his friends. On Thanksgiving Day, November 29, 1860, the most eloquent and influential preacher of the South, Dr. Benjamin Morgan Palmer, who that same year had been unanimously elected by the General Assembly of the Presbyterian Church to a chair at Princeton Theological Seminary, preached a sermon in his pulpit, the First Presbyterian Church of New Orleans, on Ps. 94:20: "Shall the throne of iniquity have fellowship with thee?" In this powerful sermon, Dr. Palmer took the position that every

nation has a particular mission and destiny to work
out, and that the mission of the South was "to con-
serve and perpetuate the institution of domestic
slavery as now existing." In the discharge of this
trust, "should the madness of the hour appeal to the
arbitration of the sword, we will not shrink even
from the baptism of fire. If modern crusaders stand
in serried ranks upon some Plain of Esdraelon, there
shall we be in defense of our trust. Not till the last
man has fallen behind the last rampart shall it drop
from our hands, and then only in surrender to the
God who gave it."

On that same Thanksgiving Day, 1860, Beecher
preached his sermon "Against a Compromise of
Principle." The sermon answered the proclamation
of the Democratic mayor of New York City, Fer-
nando Woods, in which he called the citizens of
New York to meet together for prayer and thanksgiving, although "the country either in its political,
commercial, or financial aspects, presents no feature
for which we should be thankful." This Woods followed up with the suggestion that in their Thanksgiving Day prayers, the people ask judgment upon
those who had brought the nation to so low a state.
This extraordinary proclamation Beecher answered

with one of his most thundering sermons. In the conclusion he said: "Shall we then compromise? We are told that Satan appears under two forms—that when he has a good fair field, he goes out like a lion, roaring and seeking whom he may devour; but that when he can do nothing more in that way, he is a serpent and sneaks in the grass; and so is slavery, open, bold, roaring and wrecking; or it is slavery snaking in the grass and calling itself compromise. It is the same Devil under either name."

A comparison of these two powerful sermons by the representative preachers of the North and South will deliver one from the delusion that the Civil War was brought on by a few irresponsible, political firebrands, North and South. Beecher told the truth about the great struggle when he said in that Thanksgiving Day sermon, "There is a divine impulsion in this; those who resist and those who strive are carried along by a stream mightier than mere human volition."

There is an interesting tradition, but difficult of confirmation, that in one of the darkest hours of the Civil War, Lincoln paid a secret visit to Henry Ward Beecher, in his home at Brooklyn, that he might have his hand strengthened in God.

In 1863, Beecher went to England, and in Birmingham, Manchester, Lancaster, Liverpool, Glasgow, delivered a series of great addresses which helped to change the sentiment of the British people toward the North. Never did a man face such hostile and savage audiences, yet in an extraordinary way he mastered them and won not only their attention but their applause. An example of his power over such an audience was seen when he spoke at Liverpool. He was constantly interrupted and could hardly make any headway with his speech. At last one man in the audience, amid great cheers from the crowd, cried out, "Why didn't you put down the rebellion in sixty days as you said you would?" Beecher waited for a little until the crowd became silent in their eagerness to hear his reply, and then hurled back at them, "We should, if they had been Englishmen." After a moment's amazement and anger, the English love of fair play prevailed and the hostile throng cheered him to the echo.

On the fourth anniversary of the firing on Fort Sumter, April 14, 1865, Beecher delivered the oration at the raising of the flag over the ruined fortress. Never did a preacher have such a pulpit. Standing on the blackened ruins of Fort Sumter, he could survey the desolate city of Charleston, the cradle of secession, and with the tragic memories of the Civil War behind, and the hope of victory now filling every Northern heart, the great preacher poured forth a hymn of thanksgiving and rejoicing such as has seldom fallen from the lips of man. In the conclusion of his address, Beecher said: "From this pulpit of broken stone we speak forth our earnest greetings to all our land. We offer to the President of these United States our solemn congratulations that God has sustained his life and health under the unparalleled burdens and sufferings of four bloody years and permitted him to behold this auspicious consummation of that national unity for which he has waited with so much patience and fortitude, and for which he has labored with such disinterested wisdom."

Within a few days Beecher was standing in his own pulpit to preach Lincoln's funeral sermon. He took his text from the passage in the book of Deuteronomy, where Moses goes up to the top of Pisgah and is permitted to view the Promised Land, but forbidden to go over thither. It was a grand, prophetic, and extraordinarily appropriate text. In the conclusion of the sermon, with prophetic vision,

Beecher said: "And now the martyr is moving in triumphal march, mightier than when alive. The nation rises up at every stage of his coming. Cities and states are his pallbearers and the cannon beats the hour with solemn progression. Dead! Dead! Dead!—he yet speaketh! Is Washington dead? Is Hampton dead? Is David dead? Is any man dead that was ever fit to live? Disenthralled of flesh and risen to the unobstructed sphere where passion never comes, he begins his illimitable work. His life is now grafted upon the infinite, and will be fruitful as no earthly life can be. Pass on, thou that hast overcome!

"Four years ago, O Illinois, we took from your midst an untried man, and from among the people. We return him to you a mighty conqueror, not thine anymore, but the nation's; not ours, but the world's. Give him place, ye prairies; ye winds that move over the mighty places of the West, chant his requiem; ye people, behold a martyr whose blood as so many articulate words pleads for fidelity, for law, for liberty."

In the year 1871, and until 1875, the great preacher passed through the fiery furnace of trial. One of his young friends and protégés was Theodore

Tilton, a brilliant newspaper man who, through Beecher's influence, had been made assistant editor and afterward editor in chief of *The Independent*. Tilton's views as to marriage and religion made it necessary for the publishers of *The Independent* to dismiss him from the editorship. At the same time, on the advice of Beecher, Mrs. Tilton separated from her husband. These seem to have been the incidents which embittered Tilton toward his one-time benefactor and made him resolve, as he expressed it, "to strike Mr. Beecher to the heart." Scandalous underground stories affecting Beecher's character had been in circulation for some time, but it was not until June, 1874, that Tilton, made a public charge against Beecher. Beecher then asked a committee of six from his church to investigate the charges. After long investigation the committee reported that they found nothing in the evidence "that should impair the perfect confidence of Plymouth Church or the world in the Christian character and integrity of Henry Ward Beecher." In August of that year Tilton filed a complaint charging Beecher with adultery with Mrs. Tilton and demanding $100,000 damages. It was one of the most celebrated trials in the history of America. The jury failed to agree on a verdict, the vote being nine to three in favor of the defendant. A year afterward two hundred and forty-four representatives of the Congregational Church examined the charges and declared Beecher innocent of all that was charged against him. During these terrible years, Beecher continued to preach in his pulpit and some of his most spiritual sermons date from that period. His congregation showed their confidence in him by presenting him with $100,000 to pay the expenses of his trial.

To assist in defraying these costs, Beecher went on the lecture platform and great multitudes heard him in all parts of the country. His last sermons were preached in Plymouth Church, February 27, 1887.

Two incidents on this last Sunday at his church reveal on the one hand his sense of humor, his playfulness, and on the other hand his pathos and deep-thoughted seriousness. As he entered the church on this last Sunday, he went up to one of his old friends, one of the ushers, with a request for a seat. Adapting himself to Beecher's facetious mood, the usher said, "If you wait here until the pewholders are seated, I will try to accommodate you." "Could I get a seat in the gallery?" said Mr. Beecher. "You might try in the upper gallery," answered the usher. "But," said Beecher, putting his hand to his ear, "I am a little hard of hearing and want a seat near the pulpit." The next moment he was in his pulpit chair with the hymnbook in his hand. At the close of the evening service, Beecher lingered for a little while listening to the choir as they practiced an anthem to Faber's "Hark! Hark, My Soul! Angelic Songs Are Swelling." As he started to go out he said to those near him, "That will do to die on." A friend at his side said, "Will it not do to live on, Mr. Beecher?" But the preacher answered quickly, "That is the way to die." As he passed out of the church he saw standing near the register, for it was a cold February night, a little girl about ten years of age and her brother, five years old, who for some weeks had been coming to the church on Sunday evenings. Beecher stopped when he saw them and, putting his hand on the little boy's head, stooped down, and kissed him, saying, "It is a cold night for such little tots to be out." Then he walked to the door with the children on either side of him. A beautiful conclusion to a ministry that defended the weak and the helpless, the great preacher walking out into the night with his arms around two nameless waifs!

It is a mistake to think of Henry Ward Beecher

as just a public oracle, and a prophetic voice calling for righteousness in national affairs. He was indeed that, but he was far more than that. He was a deep interpreter and an eloquent proclaimer of the love of God in Christ Jesus. A review of his published sermons shows that comparatively few of them dealt with public questions. The topics are in the highest sense spiritual and Biblical.

Speaking to the Yale students on the question of the pulpit and public affairs, Beecher said: "You have a duty to speak on all these things. There is not so broad a platform in the world as the Christian pulpit, not an air so free as the heavenly air that overhangs it; you have a right and a duty to preach on all these things, but if you make your ministry to stand on them, it will be barren. It will be rather a lectureship than a Christian ministry. It will be secular and will become secularized. The real root and secret power, after all, in the pulpit, is the preaching of the invisible God to the people as an ever present God."

The great evangelist Dwight L. Moody came to Beecher in 1875 and asked him to give up his pulpit and go into an evangelistic campaign for the conversion of the world. "We two, working together,"

said Moody, "could shake the continent as it never
has been shaken before." This proposition made its
appeal to Beecher. And what a combination that
would have been! But Beecher was wise enough to
see that it was an impossible combination: "Mr.
Moody and I could not possibly work together in
such a mission. He believes that the world is lost,
and he is seeking to save from the wreck as many
individuals as he can. I believe that this world is to
be saved, and I am seeking to bring about the Kingdom of God on earth." These two conceptions of
Christianity and the work of the Church are, after
all, not so far apart as Beecher at the time may have
thought. In the light of the Scriptures, and in the
light of human history and the history of the
Church, Moody's conception seems to be the sounder
one; yet the preacher who would bring in the Kingdom of God on earth has his place and his work.
But Beecher did not truly describe his own position when he contrasted his view of the Kingdom
of God with that of Moody. No one can read his
sermons or read his prayers and not realize that
Beecher had a sublime and beautiful conception of
the Christian life as something far above the social
relationships and far above social justice even. With

psalmist, prophets, apostles, martyrs, and saints, Beecher knew that the Christian life in its highest form and attainment is the life which is "hid with Christ in God." Always impulsive, Beecher was ofttimes inconsistent and contradictory in his theology. His espousal of the hypothesis of evolution and with it what often appears to be a denial of the fundamental fact of human nature, the Fall of man, raised doubts as to his loyalty to the gospel and the Scriptures. The conclusion one will reach after a study of his sermons is that none of these views ever dimmed for Beecher that beautiful experience he had as a youth on that May morning in the Ohio woods when, as he says, "it pleased God to reveal to my wandering soul the idea that it was his nature to love a man in his sins for the sake of helping him out of them."

In 1871 Beecher delivered the first lectures in the now celebrated Yale Lectures on Preaching. This was a great contribution to the literature of the life and work of the ministry.

Undoubtedly, one of the secrets of Beecher's magnetism and power as a speaker was his great vitality and his overflowing animal spirits. Not long before his death, someone asked him if he were going to

Europe for his health, and he replied, "I already have more health than I know what to do with." Beecher was slightly under six feet and powerfully built. His general appearance suggested great physical strength. He had a noble forehead, "bearing witness to his intellect, a dome crown bearing witness to his reverence and his benevolence, a broad back of head bearing witness to the force and strength of his will, and heavy eyebrows indicating power of observation." He took good care of his body and of his health, and was a sound sleeper. Saturdays were always given to rest and recreation, on the theory that it is "better to rest before one's work as a preparation than after one's work as a recuperation from it." Dr. Henry C. Fish thus describes the appearance of Beecher: "The nose is a Doric column, full of strength, simplicity, majesty. The mouth is sensuous and firm, and carries in repose the set which one sees in the portraits of Washington. The forehead has no bumps; it is full, round, and flowing. All the lines of Beecher's face flow into one another. There are no breaks."

Beecher was frequently humorous, but naturally, spontaneously so, in his preaching. Even when passing through the Gethsemane of the Tilton trial he

could joke with his lawyers. When they called on
him to consult with him and apologized for coming
on a Sunday afternoon, Beecher said—and this was
as near as he ever came to an admission that there
had been anything even indiscreet in his conduct:
"We have it on good authority that it is lawful to
pull an ass out of the pit on the Sabbath Day. Well,
there never was a bigger ass or a deeper pit!"

In his early years in Indiana, Beecher wrote his
sermons after careful preparation, but he found that
when Sunday came he was not able to preach these
sermons with any effectiveness or with any joy.
"Sometimes," he says, "I would find that after working a subject up all the week something else would
take possession of me on Saturday and I would have
to preach it on Sunday to get rid of it. I felt ashamed
and mortified and began to fear that I was on the
way to superficiality. I made many promises that if
God would help me I would make my sermons a
long time beforehand. I kept on making promises
and breaking them and the older I grew the worse
I grew, and finally, in spite of prayers and resolutions, I had to give it up and prepare my sermons
mostly on Sunday morning and Sunday afternoon.
But then you must recollect that this was accom-

panied by another habit, that of regular study and continual observation. I do not believe that I ever met a man on the street that I did not get from him some element for a sermon. I never see anything in nature which does not work toward that for which I give the strength of my life. The material for my sermons is all the time following me and swarming up around me. I am tracing out analogies which I afterward take pains to verify."

Beecher's preaching, like that of most great preachers, was topical, rather than textual or expository; but in his early days he had been a careful student of the New Testament and in his preaching he constantly drew on his wide knowledge of the principles of the New Testament. He likened much of the textual and expository preaching to a man who takes a text and swings on it as a man who swings to and fro on a gate, whereas his plan was to use the text as a gateway and entrance. Beecher's pockets were generally filled with letters, on the back of which he had jotted down sermon thoughts as they had struck him. Lyman Abbott, who was closely associated with him as a young man at Plymouth Church, relates how Beecher described to him his method of preparation. "I have," he says, "half a dozen or more topics lying loose in my mind through the week. I think of one or another as occasion may serve, anywhere, at home, in the street, in the horse-car. I rarely know what theme I shall use until Sunday morning. Then after breakfast I go into my study as a man goes into his orchard. I feel among these themes as he feels among the apples to find the ripest and the best. The theme which seems most ripe I pluck. Then I select my text, analyze my subject, prepare my sermon, and go into the pulpit to preach it while it is fresh."

For a time he would write out the introduction and the earlier portions of the sermon; but as the time for the service grew near the notes grew more abbreviated, and finally, almost at the sound of the bell, he would snatch up his sermon, hurry over to the church and up to the pulpit, drop his felt hat by the side of the chair, put the notes on the table beside him, and when the time for the sermon came, with the notes on the open Bible, he would read in a rather low voice the first few pages, and then throw his manuscript aside as he was caught up by the spirit of the occasion.

Incredible and miraculous as this method of pulpit preparation seems to us, it will be remembered that another great preacher and a contemporary of Beecher, Charles Spurgeon, followed much the same method. Theodore Cuyler tells of leaving Spurgeon on a Saturday at six o'clock, when Spurgeon assured him that he had not yet selected a text for the next day's discourse. "I shall go down into the garden presently, and arrange my morning discourse and choose a text for that and the evening, then tomorrow afternoon before preaching I will make an outline of the second one." Spurgeon never composed a sentence in advance, and rarely spent over half an hour laying out the plan of the sermon.

Speaking of other ministers and how some of them are burdened rather than exalted by their sermons, Beecher said: "Few men there are who are upborne and carried forward by their sermons. Few men ascend as the prophet did in a chariot of fire. The majority of preachers are consciously harnessed, and draw heavily and long at the sermon which tugs behind them." But what strikes one about the preaching of Beecher, even in the printed sermon, and which always impressed those who heard him preach, was that here was a preacher who ascended as Elijah did in a chariot of fire. His sermon was not something that he was dragging behind him, but something that was lifting him triumphantly heavenward.

Whoever reads the sermons or speeches of Beecher will be amazed at the spontaneous discharge of his mind and soul. As Theodore Parker said of him: "Other preachers have tanks, barrels of rain, well water, but on their premises is no spring and it never rains there. A mountain spring supplies Mr. Beecher with fresh, living water." In this respect America has never produced a preacher like Beecher. Perhaps in all its history the Christian Church has never produced a preacher of such spontaneous and overwhelming power as Henry Ward Beecher. His sermons are marvelous outpourings of a great Christian heart and mind and personality. They astound one with their combination of intense and yet simple humanity, glorious imagination, glowing rhetoric, and sweetness of intellect.

Like nearly all the great preachers, Beecher quoted hardly at all. I do not remember any prose quotations. He evidently regarded such, as Brooks said he did, as evidence of undigested knowledge. In all his printed sermons I have come across just one poetic quotation, and that is Charles Wesley's beautiful hymn on Jacob wrestling with the angel, beginning, "Come, O thou Traveler unknown."

One of the greatest things about Beecher's ministry was his extemporaneous, spontaneous, and beautiful pulpit prayers, in which he brought his congregation before the throne of grace and lifted them into fellowship with God. In these prayers he strikes every chord in the heart of spiritual longing and desire.

In his father's home at Litchfield, Beecher had for a companion an aged Negro, Charles Simms. This godly Negro had great influence on Beecher's life. They occupied the same room and Beecher was introduced to the joy and power of prayer by listening to this aged Negro pray before he went to bed. "Every night he would set the candle at the head of his bed and pray and sing and laugh, and I bear record that his praying made a profound impression on my mind. I never thought whether it was right or wrong—I only thought: How that man does enjoy it! What enjoyment there must be in such prayers as his! I gained more from that man of the idea of the desirableness of prayer than I ever did from my father or mother. My father was never an ascetic. He had no sympathy with anything of a mawkish sentiment. Yet this poor man, more than he, led me to see that there should be real, overflowing gladness and thanksgiving in prayer."

Speaking about this, Beecher said: "I think the most sacred function of the Christian ministry is praying. I can bear this witness that never in the study in the most absorbed moments, never on the street in those chance inspirations that everybody is subject to when I am lifted up highest, never in any company where friends are the sweetest and dearest, never in any circumstances in life is there anything to me so touching as when I stand in ordinary good health before my great congregation to pray for them. Hundreds and hundreds of times as I rose to pray and glanced at the congregation, I could not keep back the tears. There came to my mind such a sense of their wants, there were so many hidden sorrows, there were so many weights and burdens, there were so many doubts, there were so many states of weakness, there were so many dangers, so many perils, there were such histories, not world histories, but eternal world histories. I had such a sense of compassion for them, my soul longed for them, that it seemed to me that I could scarcely open my mouth to speak for them. And when I take my people and carry them before God and plead for them, I never plead for myself as I do for them—I never could. There is no time that Jesus is so crowned with glory as then. There is no time that I get so far into heaven. I can see my mother there. I see again my little children. I walk again arm in arm with those who have been my companions and co-workers. I forget the body. I live in the spirit, and it seems as if God permitted me to lay my hand on the very Tree of Life and to shake down from it both leaves and fruit for the healing of my people, and it is better than a sermon; it is better than any exhortation."

This noble passage is at once a beautiful evidence of the high spirituality of Beecher and a picture of the joy he took in his pulpit work, and also a splendid illustration of his moving style as a public speaker. Perhaps no one preacher ever got such joy out of his own preaching as Beecher did, and when a preacher gets joy out of preaching it is fairly certain that the people will also. He tells how in his early years in Indiana he was often discouraged and disheartened, and would come home resolved to quit the pulpit and become a farmer, or anything but a preacher. But that passed completely away with his new and free method of preaching, and he thus records the joy that he got out of his pulpit work:

"I have seen a great deal of life and all of its sides. I have had youth and middle age and now I am an old man. I have seen it all and I bear witness that while there are single moments of joy in other matters that perhaps carry a man up to the summit of feeling, yet for steadfast and repetitious experience, there is no pleasure in this world comparable to that which a man has who habitually stands before an audience with an errand of truth which he feels in every corner of his soul and in every fiber of his being, and to whom the Lord has given liberty of utterance, so that he is pouring out the whole manhood in him upon his congregation. Nothing in the world is comparable to that. It goes echoing on in you after you get through. Once in a while I preach sermons that leave me in such a delightful state of mind that I do not get over it for two days and I wonder that I am not a better man. I feel it all day Sunday and Monday, and there is not an organ in the world that makes music so grand to me as I feel in such supreme hours and moments."

Beecher's whole message and theology was love: God's love to man and the Christian's love for his fellow man. Nearly all his texts were taken from the New Testament. In the volumes of his printed sermons there are only twenty-nine texts from the Old Testament, but two hundred and twenty-four from the New Testament. His sermon, "The Nature of Christ," on the texts: "Wherefore in all things it behoved him to be made like unto his brethren," Heb. 2:17, and, "Let us therefore come boldly unto the throne of grace, that we may obtain mercy, and find grace to help in time of need," Heb. 4:16, gives us what is perhaps the best summary to be had of his theology and his way of preaching. He was convinced that there had been too much defining and refining of the great Christian truths and not enough of the personal, sympathetic, and loving Christ.

He describes a man coming to him and telling him that his mother, "who bore me and hovered over all my infant days and tenderly loved me to the last," is dead. "When you do that," he says, "you

121

open the floodgates of sympathy in my soul." Then
he describes a physician sitting down by his side and
explaining to him, in the form of an anatomical
lecture, the causes of his mother's death—all about
the valvular system, the bony system, the muscular
system, the nervous system. "That," he says, "will
not move him at all." But when a man comes to him
and tells him that his mother is dead, "that she
prayed for me and she died exclaiming: 'My son!
O my son!' you open the floodgates of sympathy in
my soul." By this comparison and contrast, he means
to point out the difference between the rationalistic
and logical statements about God and redemption,
and the human and personal statement. "Away with
your barbaric notions! Away with the idea of mar-
shaled forces! Away with the thought of imperial
coercions! Greater love hath no man than this that
a man lay down his life for his friend. Tell me what
that means? All that I want to know is that the heart
of God is a heart that yearns for men, that it is a
paternal heart by which the universe is to be lifted
up and saved. I do not stop to ask what is the relation of the suffering of the Lord Jesus Christ to
divine law; neither do I stop to ask what its relation is to the moral government of the universe;

nor do I stop to ask what is its relation to the teaching of the Old Testament. I can say of these scholastic discussions, 'They have taken away my Lord, and I know not where they have laid him.' But yes, I do know where they have laid him. They have laid him under the dry bones of philosophy. They have covered him up with slavish systems which impose upon men the performance of certain duties, the observance of given forms and ceremonies, and obedience to certain rules, as the conditions of their salvation. . . . 'Come boldly unto the throne of grace, that we may obtain mercy, and find grace to help in time of need.' O throne of iron, from which have been launched terrible lightnings that have daunted men! O throne of crystal, that has coldly thrown out beams upon the intellect of mankind! O throne of mystery, around which have been clouds and darkness! O throne of grace, where He sits regnant, who was my Brother, who has tasted of my lot, who knows my trouble, my sorrow, my yearning and longing for immortality! O Jesus, crowned not for thine own glory, but with power of love for the emancipation of all struggling spirits— thou art my God, my God!"

That was Beecher to the end: a great, loving

heart, still feeling to the last day he preached the thrill of that beautiful May morning in the Ohio woods, when it was revealed to his wandering soul that it was God's nature "to love a man in his sins for the sake of helping him out of them."

PHILLIPS BROOKS

Phillips Brooks

ON A stone over a grave in Mt. Auburn Cemetery, Boston, is cut this verse from the Gospels: "O woman, great is thy faith: be it unto thee even as thou wilt." That was the inscription which Phillips Brooks chose for his mother's grave. She was a woman worthy of that high praise. Writing once on the subject of how great men frequently have undistinguished, and sometimes good-for-nothing, sons, Phillips Brooks attributed it to the fact that there was a weakness on the mother's side. Certain it is that nearly every great preacher of the Word of God had a mother who was great in faith.

Mary Ann Phillips came of a distinguished New England line. The Phillipses were the founders of Phillips Exeter Academy, Phillips Andover Academy, and the Andover Theological Seminary. In 1833 Mary Ann married William Gray Brooks, who became a merchant in Boston, where Phillips Brooks was born, December 13, 1835, the second of six sons, four of whom entered the ministry. The Brooks family had embraced the Unitarian movement in New England, and at first Mary Ann Brooks went with her husband to the First Unitarian Church of Boston, where Phillips Brooks was baptized. When he was about to be ordained a bishop in 1891, it was suggested that he submit himself to what was called "hypothetical" baptism, on the ground that it was not certain that when he was baptized in the Unitarian Church water had been used, or that he had been baptized in the name of the Trinity; but he refused to submit himself to rebaptism. His mother was not at all satisfied in the Unitarian Church, and when Phillips Brooks was four years of age the family identified itself with St. Paul's Episcopal Church, where Dr. Vinton was the pastor. A few years later the father was confirmed as a member of the Episcopal Church. Through the influence of his godly and pious mother, Phillips Brooks's home training was of the highest order. There was family worship morning and evening, and when he entered Harvard the son was able to repeat two hundred hymns that he had learned on Sunday afternoons at home.

At the age of fourteen Brooks entered the Boston Latin School, where he was distinguished for little except his extraordinary height, five feet eleven inches. When he was sixteen years of age he entered Harvard College, where so many of his ancestors had been before him. A distinguished group of men were then on the small faculty of Harvard; among them were Asa Gray in botany, Agassiz in science, Felton in the classics, and Longfellow in literature. The president of the college during most of Brooks's stay was Dr. James Walker. Walker was a Unitarian, but of the orthodox brand of Unitarians, and his sermons were more orthodox than the sermons of many so-called evangelicals and Trinitarians today. The celebrated Senator from Massachusetts, George F. Hoar, used to hear Walker preach when he was at Harvard. He records after the lapse of sixty years this impression of Walker as a preacher: "The ticking of the clock in the college chapel was inaudible when the chapel was empty; but it ticked out clear and loud upon the strained ears of the auditors who were waiting in the pauses of his sentences. I can remember his sermons now. They are admirable to read, although like other eloquence, their life and spirit is lost without the effect of speech. There was one on the text, 'Thou shalt say No!' which no hearer, I venture to say, ever forgot to the day of his death." Brooks was certainly fortunate in being at Harvard at a time when he could hear sermons by a preacher such as Walker. There is no record of his having gone to hear one of America's mightiest preachers who was preaching at that time in the Boston Music Hall, Theodore Parker.

After his graduation from Harvard in 1855, Brooks took a post as a teacher in the Boston Latin School. There, at the very threshold of his life, he made a complete and dismal failure. When he was dismissed, the headmaster offered him the poor consolation that he had never known anyone who had failed as a schoolmaster to succeed in any other calling. The world is thankful today that Phillips Brooks failed as a schoolmaster, else he might not have influenced thousands through his power as a preacher. Another great preacher, Frederick Robertson, whose father was an officer in the British Army, and who as a boy had played about the forts at Leith, was ambitious to be an officer in the army, and was greatly disappointed when he failed to secure a commission. But it was that failure which turned him toward the ministry. God has secret blessings in his disappointments. The Spirit of Jesus would not suffer Paul to preach the gospel in Asia, where he wanted to go, or at Bithynia, which was his second choice; but these doors were closed against him only that he might come down to Troas and have his great dream of the man from Macedonia.

In the days of humiliation and mortification after his dismissal from the Latin School, Brooks went to speak with President Walker at Harvard, who encouraged him to study for the ministry. He then called on Dr. Vinton at St. Paul's Church to ask him what steps he must take to prepare himself for the ministry. When Dr. Vinton told him that he ought to be confirmed before becoming a candidate for holy orders, and that conversion was generally considered a prerequisite for confirmation, Brooks replied that he did not know what conversion meant. This shows how late he was in coming to a definite Christian experience. Fortunately, Dr. Vinton did not stand on technicalities, but encouraged him to enter the seminary of the Protestant Episcopal Church at Alexandria, Virginia, just across the river from Washington, at that time a somewhat one-horse institution.

The teaching at the seminary was inadequate compared with what Brooks had been accustomed to at Harvard, and he was so discouraged that he wrote to Andover Theological Seminary, asking about the terms of admission there. The answer was not encouraging and he remained at Alexandria for three years, much more contented in the second and third years than he had been in the first. It was while he was in the seminary that he took his first Communion by the side of his mother at St. John's Church in Washington. Shortly after he entered the seminary at Alexandria, he was taken to a students' prayer meeting. This was his first experience of a prayer meeting, and he felt somewhat ashamed as he knelt by the side of the other students and listened to their earnest petitions.

What was lacking in the curriculum in the seminary, Brooks himself supplied by his deep and wide reading and the copious notes which he made. His first sermon was on the text from II Cor. 11:3: "The Simplicity That Is in Christ." When the sermon was criticized by his classmates, as was the custom, one of them said that there was "very little simplicity in the sermon, and no Christ." Commenting on that criticism, Brooks afterward wrote, and how truly: "Its lack of simplicity and lack of Christ no doubt belonged together. Probably an attempt to define doctrine, instead of to show a man, a God, a Saviour." That is a searching homiletic comment. Where Christ as he is presented in the Scriptures is in a sermon, there also you will have simplicity.

In his last year at the seminary Brooks preached in a near-by mission church. On a Sunday afternoon in March, 1859, two strangers appeared at the little chapel of the Sharon Mission, and invited him to become the rector of the Church of the Advent in Philadelphia. Not sure as to his ability, Brooks would not accept a formal call, but agreed to serve for three months. At the end of that time, if the vestry so desired, they could give him a permanent call and he, if he so desired, was to have the liberty to withdraw. The church stood on York Avenue at the corner of Buttonwood Street. There Brooks began his ministry, July 10, 1859. He was not altogether encouraged when, walking home one Sunday evening with a vestryman, he said to him that he thought he had better withdraw at once and not wait until the three months were out. All the vestryman had to say was, "As long as you have begun, you had better stay out the time for which you were hired."

Brooks, however, was making a name and place for himself in this somewhat obscure uptown Philadelphia church. People began to come to his evening services from other churches and from other parts of the city. Those were stirring times in Philadelphia and in the country. John Brown was hanged at Charles Town in December of that year. Phillips Brooks, a kinsman of Wendell Phillips, took a strong stand on the slavery question, and his Thanksgiving Day sermons and other patriotic sermons were notable events. Other churches in other parts of the country began to invite him to become their minister; but the call which he accepted was that to Holy Trinity Church, on Rittenhouse Square, Philadelphia. Brooks had preached there for the rector, Dr. Vinton, his pastor in Boston, and when Vinton resigned the rectorship of the church in 1861 he recommended Brooks as his successor. This was a great opportunity, and Brooks commenced his ministry at Holy Trinity on the first of January, 1862. The Church of the Advent deeply resented his going, and throughout his Philadelphia ministry, and elsewhere, Brooks was annoyed with unkind criticisms and rumors, most of which originated in the resentment felt by his former parishioners in the Church of the Advent. Among the rumors was one that he had been presented with one hundred and fifty pairs of knitted slippers!

The Philadelphia pastorate at Holy Trinity from 1861 to 1869 laid the foundations of Phillips Brooks's fame and power as a preacher of the gospel. He had access to the inner circles of Philadelphia society, and among his warmest friends there was Dr. Weir Mitchell, the famous nerve specialist. Several times a week Brooks was wont to dine or visit at the home of Dr. Mitchell. Mitchell persuaded him to try to speak less rapidly in the pulpit, but the experiment was a failure, for the speed of his speech had a relation to his rate of thinking, and to slow down his speech affected his thought. During the years of his fame and power at Boston, Brooks often looked back with wistful longing to his happy years in Philadelphia. In some respects he was a lonely man, unveiling his soul and personality only in the pulpit. He never married, although frequently in his letters to his friends he expressed regret that he had not done so. In this connection we might recall the celebrated answer he gave to a rich woman who suggested to him that he would be more useful as a minister if he worked in double harness, and also added that in her case considerable of this world's goods would be thrown in to boot. Brooks wrote her, "Give your heart to the Lord, your money to the poor, and your hand to the man who seeks it." Good advice; but not always acceptable!

The same year Phillips Brooks commenced his preaching in Philadelphia, another great preacher, although of an altogether different type, T. DeWitt Talmage, began his ministry in the same city. The always generous Talmage thus wrote of Brooks at the time of his death: "My mind goes back to the time when Bishop Brooks and myself were neighbors in Philadelphia. He had already achieved a great reputation as a pulpit orator. The first time I saw him was on a stormy night as he walked majestically up the aisle of the church to which I had ministered. He had come to hear his neighbor, as I often afterward went to hear him. What a great and genial soul he was! He was a striking man that people in the street stopped to look at, and strangers would say as he passed, 'I wonder who that man is?' Of unusual height and stature, and with a face beaming with kindliness, once seeing him he was always remembered. But the pulpit was his throne. With a velocity of utterance that was the despair of the swiftest of stenographers he poured forth his impassioned soul, making everything he touched luminous and radiant. . . . We are glad that we ever knew him, that we ever heard him, and that for many years we had loved him. There were some who thought there was here and there an unsafe spot in his theology. As for ourselves, we never found anything in the man or in his utterances that we did not like. The gospel of Jesus Christ is kindness, and Phillips Brooks was as grand an exponent of that as any man we ever knew. All intelligent Christendom mourns his going. We shall not see his like again. His name will be held in everlasting remembrance."

The years just before the Civil War, during the Civil War, and immediately after the Civil War were great years for the preacher. Men's feelings were deeply stirred and their utterance was intense. Such a period kindles the zeal, expands the intellect, and stirs the imagination of the preacher. Phillips Brooks profited greatly in this grand period when he was preaching in Philadelphia. He followed the movements of the armies, sorrowed over the frequent reverses that befell the Federal armies, and rejoiced in their victories. His uncompromising ut-

terances on the subject of the conflict, his denunciation of the Episcopal Church for not taking a
stronger stand, and his ardent espousal of the cause
of the North were offensive to some of his parishioners at Holy Trinity, and not infrequently he was
paid that highest tribute which can befall a preacher,
an empty pew. But as soon as the pews were emptied
by the disaffected, they were filled by loyal and enthusiastic adherents. His ministry in Philadelphia
was spiritual and evangelical. In addition to the
Sunday services, there was the Wednesday evening
lecture and the preparatory service before the Communion, just as in the non-Episcopal churches today.

Brooks was one of Philadelphia's patriotic ministers who with spades in their hands, and led by
the celebrated Albert Barnes, of the First Presbyterian Church, appeared at the mayor's offices and
asked to be set to work on the trenches and forti-
fications around Philadelphia at the time of Lee's
invasion of Pennsylvania in the summer of 1863.
As a member of the Christian Sanitary Commission,
Brooks went down to Gettysburg and saw at first
hand something of the sorrow and tragedy of a battlefield. His sermon after the death of Abraham Lincoln was one of his greatest utterances. In this sermon he said of Lincoln: "It is the great boon of such

characters as Mr. Lincoln that they reunite what God has joined together and what man has put asunder. In him was vindicated the greatness of real goodness and the goodness of real greatness. The twain were one flesh." On July 21, 1865, in the midst of a distinguished gathering for the Harvard Commemoration, Phillips Brooks made the prayer which has been more spoken about than any of his sermons or other public utterance. No record remains of it; but it was a prayer that lifted the scholars, soldiers, and statesmen up to the throne of God. It was at this gathering that James Russell Lowell read his famous "Commemoration Ode." But what Lowell said, and Julia Ward Howe, and Ralph Waldo Emerson, and Oliver Wendell Holmes, made no impression comparable to that made by Phillips Brooks's prayer. President Eliot wrote of it: "It was the most impressive utterance of a proud and happy day. Even Lowell's 'Commemoration Ode' did not, at the moment, so touch the hearts of his hearers. That one spontaneous and intimate expression of Brooks's noble spirit convinced all Harvard men that a young prophet had risen up in Israel."

Brooks was a great traveler, both in Europe and in the Orient. The result of a trip to the Holy Land in 1865 was the beautiful Christmas carol, now so familiar in all the churches, "O Little Town of Bethlehem."

In October, 1869, Phillips Brooks began his notable ministry of twenty-two years at Trinity Church in Boston. A fire destroyed the church soon after he came to Boston, and gave him an opportunity to express his ideas of ecclesiastical architecture in the splendid new Trinity Church. For twenty-two years Brooks exerted an extraordinary sway over Boston from the pulpit of Trinity Church. In contrast with his Philadelphia ministry, he took little part now in public reform and national questions, and confined himself to the work of the pulpit. Unitarian Harvard called him to the chair of Christian ethics and as college preacher; but he declined this and other attractive offers which were made him. When he went to England he was always a welcome preacher at Westminster Abbey. His Lenten sermons at Trinity Church, New York, were long remembered by those who heard them.

In 1891 Brooks was elected bishop of Massachusetts. It must have been a surprise to his friends and followers when he accepted the office of bishop. He had openly disparaged the doctrine of apostolic succession, and was most unclerical in his attitude and in his dress. Some opposed his confirmation on the ground of unorthodoxy as to the cardinal doctrines of Christianity, and others on the ground of unorthodoxy as to the peculiar doctrines of the Protestant Episcopal Church. He had offended some by taking part in the installation services for Dr. Lyman Abbott, Henry Ward Beecher's successor at Plymouth Church, and others by his fraternizing with Unitarians in Boston. But the election was confirmed and he was consecrated in Trinity Church October 14, 1891. Just as the procession for the consecration service was about to move into the church, it was held up for a little by the reading of a protest, signed by two bishops, against his consecration.

Undoubtedly one of the chief considerations which led him to leave Trinity Church and to take the office of bishop was that the labors of a great parish had become burdensome and irksome to him, and he evidently felt the fatigue of writing every week at least one sermon of five thousand words. His career as a bishop was destined to be brief. In that brief period he seemed to take a great and high interest in his new post, and was deeply impressed with the life of a bishop, particularly with his work in consecrating young men to the priesthood. He says of one confirmation in a little church that the great popular scenes he had witnessed in England when the Guards came back from Crimea, and when Napoleon and Paris welcomed the African troops, and when Washington welcomed Grant and Sherman, were nothing compared to "the touch of the Divine I witnessed in the little church that Sunday evening, which made this man seem something more than human in the eyes of many."

Brooks preached his last sermon in the Church of the Good Shepherd in Boston on Tuesday evening, January 17, 1893. Wednesday he was laid low with a sore throat and died within a few days, January 23, 1893. He was just fifty-seven years of age. He left a lonely place against the sky. Men felt that a great spiritual light had been extinguished and that a prince and a great man had fallen in Israel.

Today in front of Trinity Church in Boston stands the statue of the great preacher. On the monument is this inscription:

"Phillips Brooks
Preacher of the Word of God
Lover of Mankind
Born in Boston, A.D. 1835
Died in Boston, A.D. 1893"

Brooks prepared for the pulpit with the greatest care. He seems never to have made even a casual or occasional address without having sketched out an analysis of what he was going to say. His plan of preparation was to make notes of Sunday's sermon on Monday and Tuesday; Wednesday he would write out the plan he was to follow. This written plan itself was considerable of a manuscript, in which he carefully blocked out the paragraphs. Then on Thursday and Friday he rapidly wrote out the sermon. The sermons were generally about five thousand words in length; but his rapid speech enabled him to deliver the sermon in the time that the usual preacher would take for a much shorter sermon. Brooks never trusted to the inspiration of the moment, and seems never to have done anything without premeditation. Sometimes he departed from his manuscript, and on occasions was powerful and stirring as an extemporaneous preacher; but extemporaneous only in the sense that he was preaching without the manuscript. As a rule his sermons were read, and read with great rapidity. His Lenten addresses at Trinity Church, New York, which made so profound an impression, were delivered extemporaneously; but every sermon had been carefully worked out long before the time of preaching.

Had we worshiped on a Sunday in Holy Trinity Church, Philadelphia, or in Trinity Church, Boston, we should have seen a man six and a half feet tall, of powerful frame, broad, sympathetic and somewhat Luther-like face, without the clerical garb or collar, come hurriedly up the pulpit steps and, almost before reaching the top of them, give out his text, and then break into a torrent of glowing and rapid speech. It is estimated that he spoke as many as two hundred and thirty-five words a minute, so rapidly that his utterance could not be caught by the most expert stenographers. Some of those who heard him said that he spoke in a monotone, which indeed was inevitable, when he spoke or read so rapidly; and that he himself, although greatly moving his hearers, seemed impassive. There was no doubt that the very physical energy of his utterance and the rapidity of his speech in themselves had a physical and mental effect upon his hearers. Speaking as a rule from his manuscript, Brooks reached no great climaxes. There was no spontaneous, geyserlike, breaking forth of the highest eloquence as in the case of Whitefield and Henry Ward Beecher. But the general spirit and tone of the sermon were exalted and superior. Sometimes, however, Brooks was able to stir the deepest emotions in his hearers. When he preached at Westminster Abbey his famous sermon, "The Candle of the Lord," Dean Stanley was found in the deanery after the sermon with the tears running down his face. He declared that he had never been so moved by any sermon that he could remember.

Brooks, like most great preachers, quoted hardly at all. Although he was himself a gifted writer of verse, I have found in his printed sermons very few poetic quotations. The divisions of his sermons are well marked, but not numbered. In his Yale Lectures on Preaching, he advises the students to have careful divisions in their sermons and to show clearly at the outset of the sermon what course it will follow and to recapitulate at the end. This habit has somewhat faded out of modern preaching, and probably to its hurt, for the average person in a congregation likes to know what a man's objective is and where he is going. Brooks realized the importance of doctrinal foundation, for he said, "No exhortation to a good life that does not put behind it some truth as deep as eternity can seize and hold the conscience." But in his own preaching and exhortation, he himself assumes, rather than declares and outlines, the great doctrinal foundations. I would describe him as a "superstructure preacher," rather than a foundation preacher.

Brooks defined preaching as "the communication of truth by man to men," and that it has in it two essential elements, truth and personality. In his lectures to the Yale students he laid great emphasis on the personality of the preacher: that he must, above all else, be a true and sincere man. That is the first essential. "No man," he said, "can permanently succeed in the ministry who cannot make men believe that he is pure and devoted." Great as a preacher, Brooks was greater as a man. Men who met him and heard him realized that they were face to face with a great spirit. He had a profound appreciation of the value of every human soul, and in his own life demonstrated the greatness and beauty of the soul. His favorite text was John 10: 10: "I am come that they might have life, and that they might have it more abundantly." That was the message which Brooks liked to declare, and of which he himself was a living incarnation. One who heard him preach in Westminster Abbey said of him, "Who could know him and remain skeptical as to the reality of that divine life which it is man's highest glory to receive?" Christ said, "The thief cometh not, but for to steal, and to kill, and to destroy: I am come that they might have life." There are so many influences, ideas, habits, associations, the nature of which and the tendency of which is to destroy and mar the soul; but Christ came to give it life. This is the life that all men need. It was the joy of Phillips Brooks to declare man's capacity for the divine life because man's soul was worth the sublime acts of the incarnation and the atonement. In the midst of their trials and discouragements Phillips Brooks comforted men by showing them that all things which happen to us in this life, if received and interpreted by the Spirit of Christ, have the power to lift up and purify the soul. He encouraged men amid their failures and follies and sins by telling them that despite their sin, by the love of Christ, by the kindly and quickening influence of the Holy Spirit, by repentance and faith, they could rise above the past and triumph over their faults and sins. He told them that they were made for eternal life, and that nothing but eternal life in Christ would ever satisfy them. "The minister," Brooks once said, "must have faith in the soul. He must know that the heart of man is not all sordid, and boldly speak to it of God, its Father, as if he expected it to answer." That was the way he preached to men, and men answered.

Phillips Brooks's most widely known sermon was

the sermon before mentioned, on the text, "The spirit of man is the candle of the Lord," Prov. 20: 27. In his introduction, the first sentence sums up the truth that underlies it: "The essential connection between the life of God and the life of man is the great truth of the world." The preacher describes a candle standing in a dark room, and how, when one comes to light it with a flickering and fitful blaze from a bit of paper, the candle catches fire and burns straight and clear and constant. The candle obeys the fire. This gives him the proposition of the sermon, that the divine fire is in the world, and man is the candle which can be kindled with that fire and thus reveal God in human life.

The first truth that he dwells upon is this fact that man can glow with the divine fire: "Certain philosophies and hypotheses would seem to rob man of his significance. From the very beginning of the Bible, at the very creation, the grand note of the centralness of man is struck. . . . The animals wait for man to name them, and this history of Eden is repeated in every new wilderness where man settles. The forest waits to catch the color of his light; the beasts hesitate in fear or anger until he shall tame them to his services, or bid them depart. The earth under his feet holds its fertility at his command and answers the summons of his grain or flower seeds. The very sky over his head regards him, and what he does upon the earth is echoed in the changes of the climate and the haste or slowness of the storms. This is the great impression which all the simplest life of man is ever creating, and with which the philosophies which would make little of the separateness and the centralness of the life of man must always have to fight."

Then comes a beautiful passage in which the great preacher makes clear that only man in this world can truly reflect and reveal God. God must reveal purpose and righteousness, and it takes personality to do that. "Only a person can truly utter a person. Only from a character can a character be echoed. You might write it all over the skies that God was just, but it would not burn there. It would be at best only a bit of knowledge, never a gospel, never something which it would gladden the hearts of men to know. That comes only when a human life capable of a justice like God's, made just by God, glows with his justice in the eyes of men, a candle of the Lord.

"If fire is put to granite, it only glows with sullen

resistance, and as the heat increases, splits and breaks, but will not yield; but the candle obeys and so in it the scattered fire finds a point of permanent and clear expression. . . . Whoever has in him the human quality, whoever has the spirit of man, has the candle of the Lord. But there can be light only where there is obedience to God."

He then shows how the great spiritual leaders of the past had illuminated the world's darkness with the light of God burning in their candles. But not only the great men, but "a poor, meager, starved, bruised life, if only it keeps the true human quality, and does not become inhuman, and if it is obedient to God in its blind, dull, half-conscious way becomes a light. The fire is the same, whatever be the human life that gives it its expression. There is no life so humble that, if it be true and genuinely humble and obedient to God, it may not hope to shed some of his light." That note of encouragement was characteristic of Brooks's preaching.

But what of men rich in attainments, well educated, well trained, who stand in the midst of their fellow men completely dark and helpless? "They built themselves for influence, but no one feels them. They kindled themselves to give light, but no one shines a grateful answer back to them. At last they die, and the men who stand about their graves feel that the saddest thing about their death is that the world is not the darker perceptibly for their dying. What does it mean? If we let the truth of Solomon's figure play upon it, is not the meaning of the familiar failure simply this: These men are unlighted candles; they are the spirit of man elaborated, cultivated, finished to its very finest, but lacking the touch of God. As dark as a row of silver lamps all chased and wrought with wondrous skill, all filled with rarest oil, but all untouched with fire, so dark in this world is a long row of cultivated men, set up along the corridors of some age of history, around the halls of some wise university, or in the pulpit of some stately church, to whom there is come no fire of devotion, who stand in awe and reverence before no wisdom greater than their own; who are proud and selfish, who do not know what it is to obey. There is the explanation of your wonder when you cling close to some man whom the world calls bright, and find that you get no brightness from him."

Then the preacher turns to something worse than a powerless or an uninfluential life, and that is a life whose influence is for evil. "There is a multitude of men whose lamps are certainly not dark, and yet who certainly are not the candles of the Lord. A nature furnished richly to the very brim, a man of knowledge, of wit, of skill, of thought, with the very graces of the body perfect, and yet profane, impure, worldly, and scattering skepticism of all good and truth about him wherever he may go. His is no unlighted candle. He burns so bright and lurid that often the purer lights grow dim in the glare. But if it be possible for the human candle when it is all made, when the subtle components of a human nature are all mingled most carefully, if it be possible that then instead of being lifted up to heaven, and kindled as a pure beam of Him who is eternal and absolutely good, it should be plunged down into hell and lighted at the yellow flames that burn out of the dreadful brimstone of the pit, then we can understand the sight of a man who is right in every brilliant quality, cursing the world with the continual exhibition of the devilish instead of the godlike in his life."

But there is still another kind of candle. It burns with the fire of God, and yet not with that fire alone. These men have kindled their lives in God's fire, but they cannot get rid of themselves. "They are

mixed with the God they show; they show themselves as well as him. . . . This is the secret of all
pious bigotry, of all holy prejudice; it is the candle
putting its own color into flame which it has bor-
rowed from the fire of God. The violent man makes
God seem violent; the feeble man makes God seem
feeble; the speculative man makes God seem like a
beautiful dream; the legal man makes God look like
a hard and steel-like law. Here is where all the harsh
and narrow part of sectarianism comes in."

Then the preacher turns to show how Christ, the
Perfect Man, burned with the true light of God.
"That was the power and richness of his life. It ab-
horred to burn with any fire that was not divine."

The sermon comes to a close with this ringing
note of appeal: "You are a part of God. You have no
place or meaning in this world but in relationship
to him. The full relationship can only be realized
by obedience. Be obedient to him and you shall
shine by his light, not your own. Then you cannot
be dark, for he shall kindle you. Then the Devil may
hold his torch to you, as he held it to the heart of
Jesus in the desert, and your heart shall be as unin-
flammable as his.

"As candles are prepared for the holy ceremonies
with anxious care, so with what care must the man

be made whose spirit is to be the candle of the Lord! It is His Spirit which God is to kindle with Himself. Therefore, the spirit must be the precious part of him. The repentance of sin and acceptance of forgiveness must be not merely that the soul may be saved from the fire of hell, but that it may be touched with the fire of heaven and shine with the love of God as the stars forever."

This sermon is characteristic of all the preaching of Phillips Brooks. The preacher is dealing with Christianity as a life. In that respect he was a prophet and forerunner of the present generation of popular preaching, the preaching which centers upon the expression of Christian principle and truth in man's life, reflecting the life which is in Christ Jesus. This is, indeed, one side of the Christian life, for if Christ reconciled us to God by his death on the cross, we are, as Paul put it, "saved by his life." The preaching of Phillips Brooks centered almost exclusively on that second part or aspect of Christian faith. His preaching, therefore, is not the highest preaching, for the redemptive truth, the cardinal truth of Christianity, is but feebly accented; but, as far as such preaching goes, Phillips Brooks's preaching of the Christian life has never been surpassed.

T. DeWITT TALMAGE

T. DeWitt Talmage

WHEN I was a senior at the University of Wisconsin, I heard Talmage lecture at the Monona Lake Chautauqua. How clearly I can see him now after the lapse of all these years! He stood well back from the edge of the platform, above the medium height, well-proportioned, a large powerful frame, frock coat with black string tie tucked under a lie-down collar, his hair gray and his face broad, human, and kindly. He commenced speaking with his eyes closed. The voice, although not melodious like Bryan's, was powerful, arresting, and stirring. He began with a description of a man riding in a buckboard over the Illinois prairies in the springtime when the flowers were blooming. It was a vivid picture of the flowers of the field sweeping the bellies of the horses as the buckboard was driven across the plains.

This went on for a minute or two. Then, opening his eyes, he leaped forward to the front of the platform, and with a mighty voice pronounced a sentence which I have not forgotten. There was something about the man that at once appealed to you. He had the air of friendliness, and also of complete command of the situation, as if there were no doubt at all that he would carry his audience with him, which, of course, he did. Many of those who formed their conceptions of Dr. Talmage from the unfriendly caricatures and criticisms in the newspapers had conceived an intense dislike for him; but that dislike generally disappeared when they saw the man and heard him speak. It was so with the renowned actor Joseph Jefferson. Jefferson and Talmage became intimate one winter during a stay in Florida. Jefferson recalled the famous sermon of Talmage against the theater, preached in the tabernacle at Brooklyn, and how he and other actors had gone to hear the sermon. "When I entered that church to hear your sermon, Doctor," said Jefferson, "I hated you. When I left the church I loved you."

Talmage was a unique and remarkable man. As his son expressed it in his memorial sermon for his father, no matter what it was that he did, he was sure to do it differently from anyone else. Talmage himself said: "Each life is different from every other life. God never repeats himself and he never intended two men to be alike." Certainly there was never another Talmage.

T. DeWitt Talmage was born January 7, 1832, at Middlebrook, New Jersey, where his father kept a tollgate. He was the youngest of eleven children. Four of the sons became honored ministers of the gospel, one of them, John Van Nest, a distinguished missionary in China. His father and mother, like the parents of John the Baptist, were "both righteous before God" and came of a godly line. His grandparents on the Talmage side had been converted at one of Finney's evangelistic meetings. Talmage said of his mother that when she led the family prayers she would often pray, "O Lord God, I ask not for my children wealth or honor; but I do ask that they all may be subjects of thy converting grace." When Talmage was still a very young child his parents removed to a farm near Somerville, New Jersey. This farm, with the farmhouse, and the barn and the brook, and the watering trough, and the horses and the carriages, frequently appears in Talmage's sermons.

At nineteen years of age Talmage entered the
University of the City of New York, where he stud-
ied law. He then went to the New Brunswick Seminary of the Dutch Reformed Church. At the seminary he evinced the same extraordinary, original,
and somewhat sensational style of expression in
preaching as characterized him in after life. One of
his instructors said to him, after he had preached
his first class sermon, "DeWitt, if you don't change
your style of thought and expression, you will never
get a call to any church in Christendom as long as
you live."

I once talked with a classmate of Dr. Talmage
and asked him about his early impressions of the
great preacher when he was a student in the seminary. His reply was, "Exactly the same in personality and style as he was in the days of his fame.
His first sermon," he said, "was on the text, Prov.
18:24, 'There is a friend that sticketh closer than a
brother.' In the sermon he described the scene in
heaven when Christ set out on the mission of redemption. The astonished angels said to him, 'Shall
ten thousand of us weave our wings together to make
a fit chariot for thee to ride upon in thy descent to
that fallen world?' This offer Christ rejected with a

wave of his hand. The angels then exclaimed, 'Shall we bring together all the clouds of heaven and make a fit throne for thee to sit upon?' But this offer, too, Christ refused, saying, 'No, I cannot go in such a way.' And then he commanded them, 'Take off these royal robes,' and the angels reluctantly obeyed. And then he started away from them on his descent to earth without any of his royal insignia, alone, without a single attendant, and the angelic hosts, amazed, crowded out on heaven's vast balcony to see him descend, and as they gazed after him, they talked so loud together about his wonderful condescension and love for men that the shepherds of Bethlehem heard them." Anyone who is familiar with the sermons of Talmage will at once recognize him in this first sermon.

On July 26, 1856, Talmage was ordained and installed as pastor of the Dutch Reformed Church at Belleville, New Jersey, near Newark. He gave an amusing account of how on the first Sabbath he had his sermon at his side as he sat on one of the great horsehair sofas which were the pulpit style in that day. To his consternation the sermon slipped down through an opening in the back of the sofa, and while the congregation were singing the hymn be-

fore the sermon he had to get down on his hands
and knees and recover the manuscript. On another
occasion, when gas was being introduced for the
first time into the church, he planned to read an
introductory part of his sermon and then launch
out upon the great sea of extemporaneousness. But
as he drew near the end of the written part, he became terrified and prayed that the lights would fail.
His prayer was answered and the gas lamps went out,
leaving the room in darkness. He then said to the
congregation, "It is impossible to proceed." But
when he got home he felt it to be humiliating that
a man with a message from the Lord God Almighty
should be dependent upon paper mills and gas
meters. This made him resolve to strike out on a new
line of preaching without notes. As an extemporary
preacher he had few peers.

In 1859, Talmage was called to a Dutch Re-
formed Church in Syracuse, New York. There he at-
tracted some little attention, and at Hudson, New
York, delivered his first lecture, for a fee of $50. In
1862 he became the pastor of the Second Reformed
Church of Philadelphia. In this same year Phillips
Brooks began his notable ministry in Holy Trinity
Church, Philadelphia. Nothing could have been more

striking and, in a way, sensational to the Philadelphians than the pulpit style of Talmage. His preaching at once attracted great throngs. The period of the Civil War was a great age for the preacher. The times were stirring, the atmosphere was charged with electricity. A great period like that is stimulating to the intellect and imagination of the preacher. It is not strange, then, that when one calls the roll of America's famous preachers, he discovers that so many of them, Theodore Parker, Henry Ward Beecher, Matthew Simpson, Benjamin Morgan Palmer, Phillips Brooks, and DeWitt Talmage, belong to that age.

During this Philadelphia pastorate, the wife of Talmage was drowned when they were boating on the Schuylkill River.

By 1869 the fame of Talmage had gone abroad. In that year he was called to churches in Chicago, Boston, and San Francisco, and the Central Presbyterian Church of Brooklyn. He accepted the call to the depleted and faction-torn church in Brooklyn, and was installed as pastor by the Presbytery of Brooklyn, March 22, 1869. In a short time the congregations were so large that the church was not able to accommodate them. A new church, which was called the Tabernacle, was hastily built. This was destroyed by fire December 22, 1872, the first of three tabernacles to suffer such a fate. Talmage, like Beecher, held that the conventional church architecture and the pulpit arrangement were a hindrance to the preacher. Like Beecher, he had no pulpit, but a long platform. He made full use of his long platform and roamed to and fro over it, preaching with every inch of his body. The people were all seated near him, in front, around him, and above him. There is no doubt that for a direct appeal to an audience this is the best arrangement. The second Tabernacle was destroyed by fire in 1889, and the third in 1894. At this time Talmage had the largest congregation of any preacher in the world.

His unconventional manner and his sometimes extravagant statements made him the object of much ridicule and hostile attack. In 1879 he was accused before the Brooklyn Presbytery of falsehood and deceit, and of using improper methods of preaching which tended to bring religion into contempt. On all these charges he was acquitted. Talmage attributed much of his world-wide fame to the attacks that other preachers, and later, the newspapers, made upon him.

Talmage created an early sensation in Brooklyn

by his explorations into the night life of New York, accompanied by elders of his church and police officers. This gave him material for some of his most graphic descriptions. They remind one of another great pictorial preacher, Thomas Guthrie, of Edinburgh, and his moving descriptions of the submerged populace of Edinburgh.

Like most great preachers, he preached to the heart. He made it the aim in his preaching always to help somebody. He said: "A preacher should start out with the idea of helping somebody. Everybody wants help except a fool."

One of the secrets of his success, undoubtedly, lay in the fact that he had a warm heart. There was a deep vein of sentiment in him. He would never allow the spot on the barn door at East Hampton, Long Island, where his deceased son, DeWitt, had carved his initials to be painted over or changed. He had unshaken faith in the Bible. "Science and revelation," he said, "are the bass and soprano of the same tune." Colonel Ingersoll, with his attacks on the Bible, Talmage likened to a grasshopper on a railway line when the express comes thundering along.

The preacher kept himself in physical condition

by walking every day of his life; every day except Friday, Saturday, and Sunday, regardless of the weather, he covered five miles. His physical energy was inexhaustible. He said Gladstone was the only man he ever met who walked fast enough for him.

After the destruction of his third Tabernacle, Dr. Talmage became the Associate Pastor of the First Presbyterian Church of Washington. For his installation sermon he preached one of his most picturesque discourses, "All Heaven Is Looking On," from Heb. 12:1, "Compassed about with so great a cloud of witnesses."

After four years as pastor in Washington, he resigned his charge in 1899 and until his death in 1902 gave himself to lecturing, preaching, and editorial work. He was taken ill on a trip to Mexico and returned to his home in Washington, where he died April 12, 1902.

Talmage was a great traveler. He found it easy to meet distinguished men, and even the crowned heads of Europe. Through the *Christian Herald*, he loaded a ship with food supplies for the victims of a famine in Russia.

A remarkable thing about the career of Talmage is that from the time he began to draw great crowds in Philadelphia until his death in 1902, almost forty years, his popularity never waned. One of the secrets of his appeal undoubtedly was his invincible optimism. This radiated not only in his written and spoken sermons, but in his personal appearance, his expressive and mobile and ever smiling mouth. When he commenced his ministry he was not strong. Now and then he would overhear people say, "Ah, he is not long for this world." This made him resolve that never in meeting other people or in conversation with them would he say anything that was depressing. He was a great optimist. He believed that there was as great a number of people out of the Church as in it who followed the teachings of Christianity. It was in keeping with this invincible optimism that the last sermon that he wrote was a sermon on thanksgiving, Ps. 33:2: "Sing unto him with the psaltery."

Although not a doctrinal preacher at all, Talmage was true to the great evangelical doctrines of Christianity, and all his sermons, while they do not set forth or analyze those doctrines, are radiant with their light. He was brought to a decision for Christ by an evangelist, Truman Osborne, who was visiting the Talmage home. Osborne asked Talmage's father if all the children were Christians. His father told him that all were Christians but DeWitt. Then Osborne, looking into the fireplace, told the story of the Lost Sheep. It was this that brought Talmage into the fold.

One of the most far-reaching features of Talmage's ministry was his printed sermons. Looking one day at a pile of sermons that he had written and preached, he said to his wife, "God must have some other use for these sermons, and intend them for others than just those who heard me preach them." This conviction led him to make the arrangements for the weekly publication of his sermons.

A contributory cause also was the visit to Talmage of a young man, who afterward became eminent as a lawyer. He told Talmage that he was studying law in a distant city and that he must give up his studies unless he could be permitted to take down the sermons through his skill as a stenographer and arrange for their sale. At the time Talmage declined. But after some months had passed he began to reflect that it would be too bad if this brilliant young man was not able to get a legal education. He then allowed the young man to take down the sermons. Within three weeks from all over the United States requests began to come in for the sermons. They were published weekly by as many as three thousand, five hundred newspapers, and by this means Talmage spoke to a greater multitude than had any preacher of Christianity up to that time. Thousands of persons living today will remember the weekly sermons of Dr. Talmage as they appeared in the newspapers on Monday morning and in the *Christian Herald*, the weekly magazine of which he became the editor.

His style was pictorial and, like most of the great preachers, his homiletic method was topical rather than textual or expository. Illustrations came naturally to him. He said: "It has always been the question with me how to get rid of illustrations. I naturally think in metaphor." Dr. David Gregg, a contemporary in Brooklyn, thus describes his style: "He thinks in pictures and he who thinks in pictures thinks vividly. He paints with a large brush, with colors that burn and glow, and nations gather round his pictures and feel an uplift and an holy thrill." Perhaps his sermon "All Heaven Looking On" is as good an example as might be quoted of his vivid imaginative style.

The thread of the atonement ran all through his

preaching. Christ to him was central and the cross was central and cardinal. The future life and heaven were very real to him. Bidding good-by to an old friend who was on his deathbed, Talmage said, as if the man were going to leave for another city, "Give my love to my boy" (referring to his son DeWitt who had died years before). His emphasis on the grand particularities of the Christian faith was one of the secrets of his popularity with the masses of the people. Senator Beveridge, who heard him frequently, said: "The American people are tired of hearing learned and entertaining lectures delivered under the guise of sermons. They hunger and thirst for the preaching of the faith, unweakened by doubts, criticisms, or explanation, uncompromisingly delivered as Dr. Talmage gave it."

The desire to help and to save sounded in all his sermons. One of his famous themes on the text, "The people that do know their God shall be strong, and do exploits," Dan. 11:32, was "The Three Greatest Things to Do—Save a Man, Save a Woman, Save a Child." The contagious optimism and hopefulness of Dr. Talmage comes out in all his sermons. His last sermon, on "David's Harp," strikes this characteristic note of hope: "The greatest victories are yet to be gained; the grandest churches are yet to be built; the mightiest anthems are yet to be hoisted; the most beautiful Madonnas are yet to be painted; the most triumphant processions are yet to march. Oh, what a world this will be, when it rotates in its orbit a redeemed planet, girdled with spontaneous harvests, and enriched by orchards whose fruits are speckless and redundant; and the last pain will have vanished, and the last tear wept, and the last groan uttered, and there shall be nothing to hurt or destroy in all God's holy mountain!"

Most of the texts of Talmage's sermons were taken from the Old Testament. Three hundred and five of his texts are Old Testament texts and one hundred and eighty-five New Testament texts. Very often the sermons deal with some Old Testament scene or history, and this gives the preacher an opportunity to introduce his sermon with a piece of description or historical narrative. A good example of this is his well-known sermon, "The King's Wagons," on the text from Gen. 45:27, "And when he saw the wagons." The sermon commences with a description of the capital of the Pharaohs: "There were temples aflame with red sandstone, entered by gateways that were guarded by pillars bewildering with hieroglyphics, and wound with brazen serpents, and adorned with winged creatures, their eyes and beaks and pinions glittering with precious stones. There were marble columns blooming into white flower buds. There were stone pillars, the tops bursting into the shape of the lotus when in full bloom along the avenues lined with sphinx and fane and obelisk. There were princes who came in gorgeously upholstered palanquins, carried by servants in scarlet, or else drawn in vehicles with snow-white horses, golden-bitted, six abreast, dashing at full run. There were fountains from stone-wreathed vases climbing the ladder of the sun."

Thus the great word painter made the palace of Pharaoh, with all its splendor, live before his hearers. "Overdone! Too ornate!" the critic would say. But the fact is that the people enjoyed it. Talmage knew that there is a poet hidden away in the common man, and to that man he made his appeal. In these sermons on Old Testament themes, Talmage always is able to draw simple, straightforward, and helpful lessons. For instance, in this sermon on "when he saw the wagons," his two chief points are: First, that the king's wagons bring us corn and meat and many changes of garment. By this he means

God's provisions for our needs in this world. Secondly, the king's wagons bring us good news. Here he strikes the high note of immortality and union with Christ and with our departed friends. Our faith brings us word that our Joseph, Jesus, is yet alive, and that he sends messages of pardon, of peace, of life, from heaven—corn for our hunger, raiment for our nakedness. "Glorious religion! A religion made not out of death's-heads and crossbones and an undertaker's screw driver, but one abounding with life and sympathy and gladness! The king's wagons will take us to see our lost friends." Here the great preacher has a beautiful description of a stormy Sabbath at the New Jersey farmhouse where he was brought up. On those Sabbaths the children were left at home. He tells how at twelve o'clock they would go to the window to see if their father and mother were coming, and then at half past twelve, and then at one o'clock. "After a while Mary or Daniel or DeWitt would shout, 'The wagon's coming!' And then we would see it winding out of the woods and over the brook, and through the lane and up in front of the old farmhouse, and then we would rush out, leaving the doors wide open, with many things to tell them, asking them many questions."

The clearness of Talmage's homiletic style is brought out in his sermon, "The Laughter of the Bible." The sermon has five divisions: First, Sarah's laugh, or the laugh of skepticism. Secondly, David's laugh, or that of spiritual exultation: "Then was our mouth filled with laughter." Thirdly, the fool's laugh, or that of sinful merriment, or "the crackling of thorns under a pot." Fourthly, God's laugh, or that of infinite condemnation: "He that sitteth in the heavens shall laugh." And fifthly, heaven's laugh, or the laugh of eternal triumph: "Blessed are ye that weep now: for ye shall laugh."

Another interesting example of Talmage's use of Old Testament incidents is his sermon on the queen of Sheba, "Behold, the half was not told," I Kings 10:7. The sermon opened with a description of Solomon's palace. Here, as we have seen, Talmage was at his best when describing the glory and splendor of some Oriental capitol or palace. At the end of this description he says, "Why, my friends, in that place they trimmed their candles with snuffers of gold, and they cut their fruits with knives of gold, and they washed their faces in basins of gold, and they scooped out the ashes with shovels of gold, and they stirred the altar fires with tongs of gold. Gold reflected in the water! Gold flashing from the apparel! Gold blazing in the crown! Gold! Gold! Gold!"

The lessons that he draws from the visit of the queen of Sheba, are, first, that it is a beautiful thing when social position and wealth surrender themselves to God; secondly, earnestness in the search of truth, how the queen of Sheba crossed mountains and deserts to get to Jerusalem; and, thirdly, that religion is a surprise to anyone that gets it. The more we have of it, the more surprised we are, and the greatest surprise of all will be heaven. Talmage always delighted to close his sermons in heaven. There is a true homiletic in that, for most of the great hymns close there, and there the Christian enters upon the final chapter of his life.

On occasions, Talmage took one of the great doctrines and made a serious effort to expound it. An example of this is his sermon on "Vicarious Suffering": "Without shedding of blood is no remission," Heb. 9:22. The sermon opens with an account of how John G. Whittier once asked Talmage after he had given out the hymn, "There Is a Fountain Filled with Blood," at morning devotions at a hotel in the White Mountains, "Do you really believe there is a literal application of the blood of Christ to the soul?" Talmage answered, "No," and in the sermon's introduction he properly explains how the blood stands for the life. It was Christ's life which was given for our salvation.

Then follow examples of vicarious suffering: the father toiling at his business to maintain the home; a mother watching for the sixth night with her sick child; another mother giving her life in prayer and thought and loving deeds for a prodigal son; then the soldiers of the Civil War giving life for the nation; then the doctors who gave their lives caring for the sick during a plague in the South; then William H. Seward, in 1846, sacrificing his popularity to defend an idiotic Negro who had slain a whole family.

Thus he traces through all life the scarlet thread of vicarious substitution until he comes to the substitution of Christ on the cross. "Christ gathered up all the sins of those to be redeemed under his one arm and all their sorrows under his other arm and said: 'I will atone for these under my right arm. Strike me with all thy glittering shafts, O eternal Justice! Roll over me with all thy scourges, ye ocean of sorrow!' And the thunderbolt struck him from above, and the seas of trouble rolled up from beneath, hurricane after hurricane, and cyclone after cyclone, and then and there, in the presence of earth and heaven and hell, yea, all worlds witnessing, the price, the bitter price, the transcendent price, the awful price, the glorious price, the infinite price, the eternal price, was paid that sets us free."

The sermon comes to a conclusion with an account of the preacher's visit to the battlefield of Waterloo, and Marshal Ney addressing his troops as he led them on the last charge. "But our great Waterloo was in Palestine. There came a day when all hell rode up, led by Apollyon, and the Captain of our salvation confronted them alone, the Rider on the White Horse of the Apocalypse going out against the Black Horse Cavalry of Death and the Battalions of the demoniacs and myrmidons of darkness. From twelve o'clock noon to three o'clock in the afternoon, the greatest battle of the universe went on. Eternal destinies were being decided. All the arrows of hell pierced our Chieftain, and the battle-axes struck him, until brow and cheek and shoulder and hand and foot were incarnadined with oozing life; but he fought on until he gave a final stroke with a sword from Jehovah's buckler, and the

Commander in Chief of hell and all his forces fell back in everlasting ruin, and the victory is ours! And on the mound that celebrates the triumph we plant this day two figures, not in bronze or iron, or sculptured marble, but two figures of living light, the Lion of Judah's tribe and the Lamb that was slain."

Talmage's striking ability to make a Biblical scene real to his congregation is found in the introduction to his sermon, "The Wings of the Almighty": "The Lord God of Israel, under whose wings thou art come to trust," Ruth 2:12.

Scene: An Oriental harvest field, grain standing, grain in swath, grain in sheaf; at the side of the field a white tent in which to take the nooning; jars of vinegar or sour wine to quench the thirst of the hot working people; the swarthy men striking their sickles into the rustling barley, others twisting the bands for the sheaves, putting one end of the band under the arm, and with the free arm and foot collecting the sheaf; sunburned women picking up the stray straws and bringing them to the binders; Boaz, a fine-looking Oriental, gray-bearded and bright-faced, the owner of the field, looking on and estimating the value of the grain, and calculating in so many ephahs to the acre. Happy is the preacher who can make a scene as real as that to his congregation!

One of Talmage's most characteristic sermons was the first sermon he preached as pastor of the First Presbyterian Church of Washington, D. C. The subject of this sermon was "All Heaven Is Looking On," from the text Heb. 12:1, "Seeing we also are compassed about with so great a cloud of witnesses." The theme and the text gave full scope for the play of Talmage's imagination. He first describes a Roman amphitheater, with the cheering thousands, and the gladiators fighting with the beasts. The Christian fights in such an arena, surrounded by a throng of witnesses. The tigers and lions of sin come out of their dens and across the sand to attack him. One man's lion is the passion for strong drink. Every man and every woman has his or her lion or tiger. But they do not fight alone. A cloud of witnesses look down upon them.

He describes first the gallery of the angels, naming nearly all the great angels of the Bible, from the angel that swung his sword at the gate of Eden to the angel of the incarnation, and all the seraphim and cherubim of heaven. All these angels are the friends of man in his struggle with the beast.

Then comes the gallery of the prophets and the

apostles—Hosea, David, Jeremiah, Daniel, Isaiah, Peter, Paul, Moses, and Noah, all cheering the Christian on. Daniel cries out, "Thy God will deliver thee from the mouth of the lions." David, "He will not suffer thy foot to be moved." Isaiah, "Fear not: for I am with thee." Paul, "Victory through our Lord Jesus Christ." Then comes the gallery of the martyrs: Latimer, and the Theban Legion, and Felicitas, who encouraged her children while they died for the faith. Then comes the gallery of the great Christians: Martin Luther, Lyman Beecher, John Calvin, George Whitefield, and Charles Wesley, and David Brainerd, and Adoniram Judson, Isaac Watts, who sings from his gallery to the Christian struggling in the arena:

> *"Must I be carried to the skies*
> *On flowery beds of ease,*
> *While others fought to win the prize,*
> *And sailed through bloody seas?"*

Then comes the gallery of our departed friends: father, mother, children, all exhorting us to be "faithful unto death."

Talmage spoke to the average man and comforted and encouraged the average man. One of his rules for the pulpit was to remember that men need

help and to try to help them. The best example of
the sermon that helps is his famous, and perhaps
favorite, sermon on the text I Sam. 30:24: "As his
part is that goeth down to the battle, so shall his
part be that tarrieth by the stuff." This was the last
sermon preached by Dr. Talmage in an American
church. The sermon opens with a graphic description of the drunken carousal of the Amalekites who
had made a raid on Ziklag and had carried away
the women and children, among them the wives of
David. Then comes the account of David's division
of the spoil; how, in spite of the men who had gone
down to the battle, those who had guarded the camp
received an equal portion of the spoil. The preacher
relates how the earl of Kintore once said to him,
"When you get back to America I want you to preach
a sermon on the discharge of ordinary duty in ordinary places." It was this request which suggested to
Talmage this famous and helpful sermon.

He illustrates his sermon by describing the defer-
ence paid to a distinguished merchant at a fashion-
able watering place. When the confidential clerk
gets his week off, no one notices him, whether he
comes or goes, yet without such a clerk there could
be no successful merchant. Men know the names of

the presidents of the great railroads, but not the names of the faithful engineers, switchmen, flagmen, brakemen. When there has been an escape from disaster at sea, the passengers thank the captain; but the captain could have done nothing without the crew, without the engineer. Then comes a moving description of how a country family deny themselves to send a promising son to college. The hired help is discharged, sugar and butter are banished from the table. Then comes Commencement Day. The brother and son receives rounds of applause as he delivers the oration of the valedictorian; but hidden away in the back of the gallery are his old-fashioned father and mother and his sisters in their plain hats and faded shawls. They made his success possible.

Then comes a passage of encouragement for the aged. The Lord will not turn off his old soldiers any more than the French did the soldiers who fought under Napoleon. The old ministers who preached on $400 a year will have their reward in heaven.

The dominant note of Dr. Talmage's preaching was that of hope and good cheer. The conclusion of the sermon strikes that note in an unforgettable way: "Cheer up, men and women of unappreciated services, you will get your reward, if not here, here-after. When Charles Wesley comes up to Judgment and the thousands of souls which were wafted into glory through his songs shall be enumerated, he will take his throne. Then John Wesley will come up to Judgment, and after his name has been mentioned in connection with the salvation of the millions of souls brought to God through the Methodism which he founded, he will take his throne. But between the two thrones of Charles Wesley and John Wesley there will be a throne higher than either on which shall sit Susannah Wesley, who with maternal consecration, in Epworth Rectory, Lincolnshire, England, started these two souls on their triumphant mission of sermon and song through all ages. Oh, what a day that will be for many who rocked Christian cradles with weary feet, and out of a small income made the children comfortable for the winter! What a day that will be for those to whom the world gave the cold shoulder and called them nobodies and begrudged them the last recognition, and who, weary and worn and sick, fainted by the Brook Besor! Oh, that will be a mighty day, when the Son of David shall distribute the crowns, the thrones, the scepters, the dominions! Then you and I will appreciate as never before the height, the breadth, the columned, the domed magnificence of my text, 'As his part is that goeth down to the battle, so shall his part be that tarrieth by the stuff'! Hallelujah! Amen!"

WILLIAM JENNINGS BRYAN

William Jennings Bryan

THE first time I heard Mr. Bryan speak was at Madison, Wisconsin, during the Presidential campaign of 1900. About all I can remember now is the great throng that gathered, and Bryan's burning denunciation of the policy of imperialism. A reference to the college oration and speeches of that period will show how the sentiments of Mr. Bryan were echoed by the youth of that day. He was then just forty years of age, his hair black, his figure strong and upright, without the heaviness that came on in later years, his voice melodious, friendly, sometimes familiar as if in personal conversation, at other times ringing out like a trumpet.

William Jennings Bryan was born March 19, 1860, at Salem, Illinois. He was son of Judge Silas and Mariah Elizabeth Bryan. Bryan counted himself fortunate in his ancestry and in the time of his birth. He says: "I was born in the greatest of all ages. No golden ages of the past offered any such opportunity for large service. I was born a member of the greatest of all the races, the Caucasian race, and had mingled in my veins the blood of English, Irish, and Scotch. I was born a citizen of the greatest of all lands; so far as my power to prevent was concerned, I might have been born in the darkest of the continents and among the most backward of earth's peoples. It was a gift of priceless value to see the light in beloved America and to live under the greatest of the republics of history."

Bryan's father was a Baptist and his mother a devout Methodist. It was a home of "plain living and high thinking," hallowed with a family altar and with Christian prayer and song. The earliest ambition of the boy was to become a Baptist minister. The thought came to him after he had witnessed an immersion in the Christian Church at Salem. But very early his thoughts were turned toward the law, and even as a child he sat on the steps of his father's court listening to the pleading of the lawyers. His father had made a vow when desperately ill in his youth that if God spared him he would pray three times a day. He was faithful to this vow and when the bells struck the hour at noon, he would bow his head and make a prayer.

At the age of fourteen Bryan was converted at evangelistic meetings in the Presbyterian church, and in company with about seventy boys and girls of the town united with the Presbyterian Church. This event, Bryan afterward said, had more influence in his life for good than any other experience. His father was fond of the book of Proverbs and would frequently call the young Bryan to him and read a chapter and comment on it. After his father's death Bryan turned to The Proverbs and for some time read it through once a month once a year. In his political speeches he quotes from this book more than from any other part of the Bible.

Bryan's father had a high opinion of education and planned for his son to go to academy and college, and at his death left fifty calves which, when grown and sold, were to afford the money to send his son to Oxford; but at his death his debts were such that it was thought best to sell the calves, and thus Bryan did not get to go to Oxford. At an early age he was sent to the academy at Jacksonville, Illinois, where he spent two years, and then to Illinois College in the same town. This was the college that had been presided over by the celebrated Edward Beecher, a great antislavery leader, the brother of Henry Ward Beecher. At Illinois College Bryan distinguished himself in debating and oratory and took an active part in Christian work. After taking his degree at the college he read law for two years at the Union College of Law and also was a student in the office of Lyman Trumbull, a friend of his father's.

For four years, from 1883-1887, Bryan practiced law with a reasonable degree of success. He was married in 1884 to Mary Baird, the daughter of a merchant in a near-by town. Bryan relates one of his early meetings with his wife: He was in a grove practicing an oration which he was to deliver at the college. When his wife-to-be and another friend approached the woods, which was near an insane asylum, a farmer left his plow, and running out to the fence, waved his hand in warning to the young women, calling out: "Don't go in there. There's a man over there shouting and waving his hands. I think he must have escaped from the asylum!"

In 1887, Bryan moved to Lincoln, Nebraska, where he was a partner in the law firm of Talbot and Bryan. Adolphus Talbot had been in the law school with Bryan at Chicago. Bryan's circumstances at first in Nebraska must have been very straitened, for he tells us how he slept on a lounge in the office and lived on two meal tickets a day. He began to take an active part in public affairs, spoke for Chautauquas, and delivered Fourth of July speeches. In 1890 he was elected to Congress out of a normally Republican district, and re-elected in 1892. In 1894 he was an unsuccessful candidate for the Senate. He then became editor in chief of *The Omaha World Herald* and also devoted much of his time to delivering public speeches. He was interested when in Congress in the subject of bimetallism and became an enthusiastic advocate of the free-silver cause. When the Democratic National Convention met in Chicago in 1896, he was one of the best known advocates of the free-silver cause and had already been frequently mentioned as a possible candidate for the Presidency. At the time of the Convention, however, the only delegates upon whom he could count were those from Nebraska, North Carolina, and half the delegation from the Indian territory. The nationally known leader of the silver cause was Congressman Bland from Missouri. He was also the most likely nominee for the Presidency since the silver men were in a majority in the Convention. But a series of events pushed Mr. Bryan to the front and made him the candidate of the party for the Presidency.

The silver plank in the platform was written by Bryan. When the time came to debate the platform, Senator Jones asked Bryan if he would like to take charge of the debate. This was the beginning of a great opportunity. Bryan had been defeated, or baffled, in his wish to become temporary chairman and permanent chairman, and now he found himself with an even better opportunity for addressing the Convention. Senator Tillman was to close the debate with a fifty-minute speech. This was regarded by all as too long for a closing speech, and it was arranged that Senator Tillman should open the debate for the silver men and that Bryan should close it. This was another opportunity for the Nebraska delegate. In his account of the Convention and speech, Bryan quotes Webster to the effect that the three essentials for a successful speech are: eloquence, the subject, and the occasion. Bryan certainly had the occasion. The opening speech by Tillman was too bitter, and stressed too much the sectional argument—the South and the West against the East. The speakers for the gold Democrats were Senator Hill, of New York; Senator Vilas, of Wisconsin; and Governor Russell, of Massachusetts. These were able and powerful debaters. It was then that Bryan took the platform. He received an enthusiastic welcome from the silver men in the Convention. Never was there such a Convention speech and never such a Convention demonstration.

As a public speaker Bryan always laid great emphasis upon a happy and favorable introduction. He used to quote Paul's introduction to the speech on Mars' Hill as an example of what an introduction ought to be. Bryan was happy in the introduction to his most famous speech. It was as follows: "I would be presumptuous indeed to present myself against the distinguished gentlemen to whom you have listened if this were a mere measuring of abilities; but this is not a contest between persons. The humblest citizen in all the land when clad in the armor of a righteous cause is stronger than all the hosts of error. I come to speak to you in defense of a cause as holy as the cause of liberty—the cause of humanity." No one will question that this was a happy and impressive introduction. From the very start, with his clear and powerful voice reaching to the remotest parts of the great coliseum, Bryan had the enthusiastic attention of the delegates. He himself thus speaks of the memorable occasion: "I shall never forget the scene upon which I looked. I believe it unrivaled in any convention ever held in our country. The audience seemed to rise and sit down as one man. At the close of a sentence it would rise and shout, and when I began upon another sentence the room was as still as a church. The audience acted like a trained choir. In fact, I thought of a choir as I noted how instantaneously, how in unison, they responded to each point made."

The speech was extemporaneous only in respect to the arrangement of its parts, for Bryan had been covering the subject in its every aspect, advancing or answering every possible argument in his public addresses for the past few years. Even the famous peroration about the crown of thorns and the cross of gold he had used several times before, "and," he says, "recognizing its fitness for the conclusion of the climax, I had laid it away for the proper occasion." Now the great occasion had come.

We can imagine how the Convention must have

roared when, referring to McKinley, who had already been nominated by the Republican Convention, Bryan said: "How is it today? Why, the man who was once pleased to think that he looked like Napoleon—that man shudders when he remembers that he was nominated on the anniversary of the Battle of Waterloo. Not only that, but as he listens he can hear with ever-increasing distinctness the sound of the waves as they beat upon the lonely shores of Saint Helena." We can imagine too how they responded to a paragraph like this: "We have petitioned and our petitions have been scorned; we have entreated and our entreaties have been disregarded; we have begged and they have mocked when our calamity came. We beg no longer! We entreat no more! We petition no more! We defy them!" Then came the great and now famous peroration: "Having behind us the producing masses of this nation and the world, supported by the commercial interests, the laboring interest, and the toilers everywhere, we will answer their demand for a gold standard by saying to them: 'You shall not press down upon the brow of labor this crown of thorns. You shall not crucify mankind upon a cross of gold.'"

The result of this Convention speech was that Mr. Bryan was nominated the next day as the Democratic candidate for the Presidency. I can remember even now the thrill I felt when as a boy in the preparatory school I read that conclusion to the Chicago speech. Bryan and Lincoln made more use of the Bible than any other of our great American orators, and never was a more powerful use made of Bible language or Bible imagery than when Bryan drew upon the Gospel narratives of the crucifixion. Twenty-eight years afterward, driving in a taxicab with Mr. Bryan through Chicago on our way to a speaking engagement, we passed near the hall where the Convention had met. I said to him, "Mr. Bryan, I suppose you had made other speeches just as good as that speech many times before, and yet they were never heard of." "Yes," he replied. "I suppose that's true. But that Convention was my opportunity, and I made the most out of it." Then leaning his head back on the cushion of the taxicab, and with a look of reminiscence in his great eyes, he said, after a moment's silence, "And that's about all we do in this life—use or lose our opportunity."

Bryan's triumphant use of his opportunity in the Chicago Convention of 1896 made him his party's candidate for the Presidency in that year, when he polled an immense popular vote, and again in 1900, and again in 1908. The three-times candidate for the Presidency became a national figure. His view of public and world affairs was widened and deepened by a trip around the world, during which he had a visit with Tolstoy in Russia. Each regarded the other as a prophet and leader of humanity.

In the Democratic Convention of 1912, rather than support the candidate who had the support of the New York delegation, Bryan changed his vote, after a thrilling speech, to Woodrow Wilson, and thus, so far as human agents are concerned, made Woodrow Wilson the President of the United States. Bryan became the first Secretary of State under Wilson, and at once began to put into operation plans for international arbitration that had long been in his mind. The result was that thirty nations signed arbitration treaties with the United States. When the *Lusitania* was sunk Bryan, rather than dispatch the note which President Wilson had drafted to Germany, and which he was sure would result in war, resigned his post. He did this fully conscious of the storm of ridicule and obloquy that would burst upon him, and which did burst upon him in all its fury. Perhaps this act was the most courageous and noble act in the history of "The Commoner"; and, strange to say, the passing of the years since America's entry into the war has brought the conviction to not a few that it was a mistake for America to enter the conflict.

Bryan's last appearance at a Democratic National Convention was at the New York Convention of 1924 when, as a leader of the dry element of his party, he opposed the nomination of Governor Smith and also the denunciation of the Ku Klux Klan by name. Measureless abuse and insults were heaped upon him by the rabble who filled the galleries. It was at a meeting of the platform committee when they were debating the Klan issue that one of the members of the committee arose and recited The Lord's Prayer. It was then that Mr. Bryan arose and, amid a solemn hush, made what was afterward spoken of in the newspapers as his "Daybreak Prayer." The prayer was as follows:

"Our heavenly Father, we come into thy presence conscious that thou art infinite in wisdom, love, and power, while we are limited in knowledge and prone to err.

"Thou dost care for thy children, and hast promised to reveal thyself and thy will to those whose hearts are open to divine suggestion.

"We need thy counsel, Lord. We are carrying great responsibilities and dealing with mighty problems that vex and trouble us. We are subject to prejudice and passion and unconscious bias.

"Cleanse our minds from all unworthy thoughts and purge our hearts of all evil desires. Show us thy way, and help us to know what thou wouldst have us say and do and be.

"We would consecrate ourselves wholly unto thee and thy service. 'Thy kingdom come. Thy will be done in earth, as it is in heaven.'

"Help us to advance in our day and this day the brotherhood thou didst establish. May it include all mankind.

"So guide and direct us in our work today that the people of our party and of our country and of the world may be better for our coming together in this convention and in this committee.

"Bless us, not for ourselves, but that we may be a blessing. We ask in Jesus' name. Amen."

The end of his great life came the next summer, July 26, 1925, at Dayton, Tennessee, where he was assisting the prosecution in the trial of a teacher for violation of the statute forbidding the teaching of any "theory which denies the story of the divine creation of man as taught in the Bible and teaches instead that man has descended from a lower order of animals." He passed away peacefully on the Sabbath afternoon in his sleep. Although the great advocate of peace and the great leader in peace treaties, he was buried at his request in Arlington Cemetery, where soldiers and generals await the trumpet of the resurrection.

Such in brief is the personal and political history of Bryan's life. But what we are interested in in particular is his witness and teaching and preaching as a Christian man. He was the greatest Christian layman of his age. He was the greatest lay preacher in the history of America. His mighty and eloquent voice rang out with great encouragement for all those who believe in God, who believe in Christ, who believe in the Bible and in the "life everlasting." There is no parallel in American history of a man so prominent in public life who was so active and outspoken in his advocacy of Christianity as was William Jennings Bryan. The nearest approach to it would be the influence of William E. Gladstone in the public life of Great Britain; but in

American history there has been nothing like it. And certainly today more than ever before, there is a sad lack of men in our political and public life who are the open and avowed champions of the Church and of Christian ethics and Christian doctrine.

Mr. Bryan was one of the great leaders, perhaps *the* great leader, in the campaign against strong drink. He was always known as an advocate of temperance, and as early as 1910 espoused the cause of local option in his own state of Nebraska. It took courage to take such a stand, for the liquor interests announced everywhere that they would drive Mr. Bryan out of public life. In the conclusion of his speech delivered before the Nebraska State Democratic Convention in 1910, Mr. Bryan said, referring to the standard of Nebraska that he had carried in past battles: "I shall not lower it now. We never espoused a more righteous cause than that which now appeals to us. We never faced an enemy more deserving of attack than that which is attempting to corrupt our party and control our state. If a retreat is to be sounded, it must be sounded by another. I shall never do it—never! never! never!"

One of the most courageous stands made by Mr. Bryan for the cause of temperance was at the Demo-

cratic National Convention of 1920 at San Francisco. It was a "wet" convention and altogether hostile to Mr. Bryan and his prohibition principles. In
his address supporting a minority report, Mr. Bryan
said: "On the night of the sixteenth day of last January, when at the nation's capital, we celebrated
the passover from the old era to the new, I was honored by the leaders of this great cause with the
privilege of being the last speaker at the meeting. I
watched the clock, and when it was within one minute of the time when this nation would become
saloonless forevermore, I quoted a passage from the
Bible, the language in which the angel assured
Joseph and Mary that it was safe to take the young
Child Jesus back to the Holy Land—you recall the
words: 'They are dead which sought the young
child's life' (applause). When you remember that
King Alcohol has slain a million more children than
Herod ever did, what language can more appropri-
ately express the joy in the hearts of parents today
than those words, 'They are dead which sought the
young child's life'?

"Are you afraid that we shall lose some votes?
O my countrymen, have more faith in the virtue of
the people! If there be any here who would seek the

support of those who desire to carry us back into bondage to alcohol, let them remember that it is better to have the gratitude of one soul saved from drink than the applause of a drunken world."

Mr. Bryan frequently spoke an apostrophe to water which reminds one of the famous apostrophe by Judge Arrington in his *Paul Denton*. This apostrophe was often used on the platform by the great temperance orator John B. Gough. It is possible, perhaps probable, that in writing *Paul Denton*, Judge Arrington had in mind the great circuit rider Peter Cartwright. But here is Mr. Bryan's apostrophe:

"Water, the daily need of every living thing! It ascends from the seas, obedient to the summons of the sun, and, descending, showers blessing upon the earth; it gives of its sparkling beauty to the fragrant flower; its alchemy transmutes base clay into golden grain; it is the canvas upon which the finger of the Infinite traces the radiant bow of promise. It is the drink that refreshes and adds no sorrow with it. Jehovah looked upon it at creation's dawn and said, 'It is good.'"

In an address on faith, delivered to many of the colleges, Mr. Bryan speaking on faith in one's self, faith in mankind, and faith in God, said: "Do not call me a preacher for I am but a layman; yet I am not willing that the minister shall monopolize the blessings of Christianity and I do not know of any moral precept binding upon the preacher behind the pulpit that is not binding upon the Christian, whose acceptance would not be helpful to everyone." But, in the broader sense, although unordained, Bryan was a great preacher, and he could strike in a wonderful way the major chords of the Christian revelation.

One of the most notable and most repeated of his addresses was "The Prince of Peace," delivered first in 1904. Toward the end of his life he told me he had ceased to give this lecture because he had given it so many times that the delivery of it had become automatic and mechanical. The preparing and giving of such an address was suggested to him by his contact with young men and his own experience when in college of the temptation toward skepticism, when, as he expressed it, the parental and home ties are being loosened and the mind is subjected to hostile scientific hypotheses. In "The Prince of Peace," although the title does not altogether suggest the contents of the address, Mr. Bryan speaks first of the universality of the religious interests and how he would rather speak on religion than on politics, how at the age of twenty he had delivered his first political speech, but at the age of fourteen his first religious speech.

Although not at that time, 1904, when the lecture was first given, the pronounced foe of the evolutionary hypothesis that he was in later years, Mr. Bryan even then struck the great note of man's divine nature and held to the doctrine of creation: "In Genesis it is written, 'In the beginning God created the heaven and the earth,' and I can stand on that proposition until I find some theory of creation that goes farther back than the beginning. We must begin with something. We must start somewhere, and the Christian begins with God." This is a characteristic statement in that it shows how Mr. Bryan did what every minister ought to be able to do, namely, to defend Christianity upon the broad ground of common sense. After defending the Bible doctrine of creation, Mr. Bryan passes on to the question of miracles. In this again he defends miracles on the ground of common sense and common experience. "Why," he asks, "should I deny that a divine hand fed a multitude with a few loaves and fishes when I see hundreds and millions fed every

year by a hand which converts the seed scattered
over the field into an abundant harvest?"

From miracles he passes on to the question of
atonement and traces the principles of vicarious suffering through nature and history, declaring that
this law, that "he that loseth his life . . . shall find
it," is an epitome of history. Then he takes up the argument for the divinity of Christ from the beauty
and uniqueness of his person and his character. He
then speaks of the different ways in which men have
sought for peace of mind and heart, and of their
failure to find it in money or in social distinction
or upon political preferment. This can be found
only in faith in God and trust in an overruling
providence. To illustrate this he quotes Bryant's
beautiful ode "To a Waterfowl." Then comes the
passage on immortality, where he states the practi-
cal value of such a hope and, telling of a correspond-
ence with Colonel Ingersoll, contrasts the agnostic's
"I do not know," with, "I do believe." Then comes
this fine passage:

"If the Father deigns to touch with divine power
the cold and pulseless heart of the buried acorn,
and to make it burst forth from its prison walls,
will he leave neglected in the earth the soul of man,
made in the image of his Creator? If he stoops to

give to the rosebush, whose withered blossoms float upon the autumn breeze, the sweet assurance of another springtime, will he refuse the words of hope to the sons of men when the frost of winter comes? If matter, mute and inanimate, though changed by the forces of nature into a multitude of forms, can never die, will the imperial spirit of man suffer annihilation when it has paid a brief visit like a royal guest to this tenement of clay?"

Mr. Bryan was termed in his day and generation a dreamer and a visionary; yet he lived to see many of his dreams come true and enacted into law. Once at a meeting of the Presbyterian General Assembly, when a speaker somewhat sneeringly had referred to the fact that Mr. Bryan had been mistaken before, Bryan sprang to the platform, his eyes blazing with indignation, and in a voice of thunder called the roll of the measures which he had advocated and which he had lived to see become the law of the land, such as woman suffrage, prohibition, the popular election of senators, international peace and arbitration treaties, federal income tax, labor representation in the Cabinet, referendum, publicity in campaign contributions, and currency reform. It was an impressive list.

In a speech delivered at Lincoln, Nebraska, in

November, 1906, Bryan referred to the fact that
public man after public man had spoken of him
as merely a "dreamer." He said that after having
heard so many governors and senators thus describe
him, he decided to plead guilty and yet justify himself as a dreamer. He would go to the Bible as an
authority. Then he told the story of Joseph and how
he was scorned by his brethren who said, "Behold,
this dreamer cometh." After he had related the story
of how Joseph saved his people from starvation in
the famine, he said, "So I decided that it was not so
bad after all for one to be a dreamer—if one has the
corn."

> *"For a dreamer lives forever,*
> *And a toiler dies in a day."*

Mr. Bryan was a great dreamer, one of that noble
company who dream of the day, and work for the
day, when the Kingdom of God shall come and
righteousness and justice and peace shall cover the
earth as the waters cover the sea.

One of the secrets of the inspiring effect that Mr.
Bryan had upon young men was that he always
struck the note of life as an opportunity for doing
good. In his address on "Man," delivered at college

commencements, he was wont to relate the story of the choice of Hercules, how at the turning of the road he was confronted by the two maidens. One in gaudy attire offered him every kind of pleasure if he would follow her path. The other, more reserved and modest in demeanor, said to him: "Hercules, I will not deceive you. The path that I point out is full of labors, full of trials, full of difficulties; but it is a path that leads to immortality. If you seek to be beloved by your friends, you must serve your friends; if you desire to be honored by any city, you must benefit that city; if you wish to be admired by all Greece for your merit, you must endeavor to be of service to all Greece." The name of this maiden was Virtue.

Thus Mr. Bryan with that matchless eloquence and that wonderful voice—alas that it has been quenched in the smoke of death!—appealed to men to live up to the highest and make full use of life's great opportunities. One of the most impressive addresses I ever heard him give was to the students of a theological seminary. He took for his text the words of God to Abraham, "Thou shalt be a blessing." He referred to the many honors that had come to him in his public life—three times the choice of his party for the Presidency, and undiminished popularity with his people—and yet he was grateful to God most of all for the wide opportunity to do good to his fellow man. That desire and passion to do good to his fellow man is echoed in every speech that Mr. Bryan delivered, in every testimony that he made, and in every chapter of his life that he wrote. And still the story of his life awakens other men and inspires them to do good. I do not know that there is any epitaph upon his tomb yonder in beautiful Arlington Cemetery, but were I asked to write one, it would be that word of God to Abraham from which I once heard him speak: "Be thou a blessing."